100 KINDERGARTEN SKILLS

Thinking Kids®
Carson-Dellosa Publishing LLC
Greensboro, North Carolina

MW00612350

Thinking Kids®
Carson-Dellosa Publishing LLC
P.O. Box 35665
Greensboro, NC 27425 USA

ISBN 978-1-4838-3115-2

Table of Contents

Table of Contents

50 MATH SKILLS

Directions: Count the number of objects out loud. Then, color the correct number.

Directions: Circle and color one star.

Directions: Circle and color two crowns.

MATH

SKILL 2: Writing 0, 1, and 2

Directions: Count the number of objects out loud. Trace the number. Write the number.

2   2
_____   _____

0
_____   _____

1
_____   _____

2
_____   _____

2
_____   _____

1
_____   _____

0
_____   _____

2
_____   _____

MATH

Skill 2: Writing 0, 1, and 2

Directions: Color the moon. Practice writing the numeral and number word.

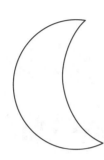

one moon

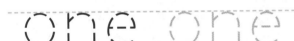

one one

Directions: Color the queens. Practice writing the numeral and number word.

two queens

2 2 2

two two

3: Counting 3 and 4

Directions: Circle the objects in each group to match the given number. Then, color the number.

3

4

4

3

3

4

Directions: Circle and color three bones.

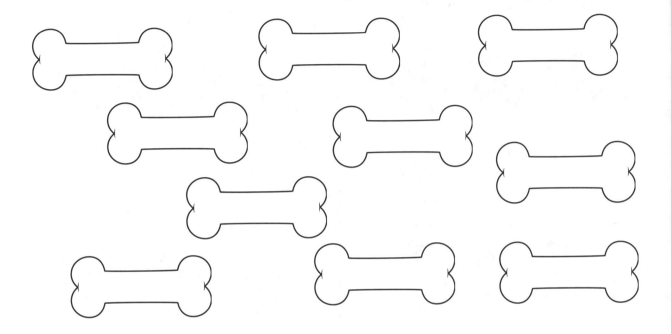

Directions: Circle and color four barns.

   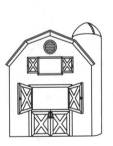 

 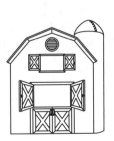   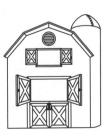

MATH

Directions: Count the number of objects in each group out loud. Trace the number. Write the number.

3   3

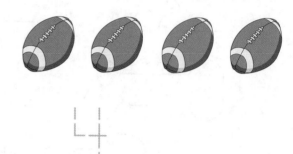

4

3

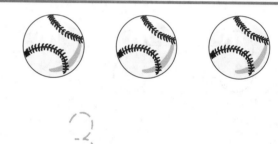

3

4

3

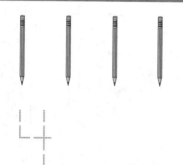

4

4

MATH

Skill **4**: Writing 3 and 4

Directions: Color the dogs. Practice writing the numeral and number word.

three dogs

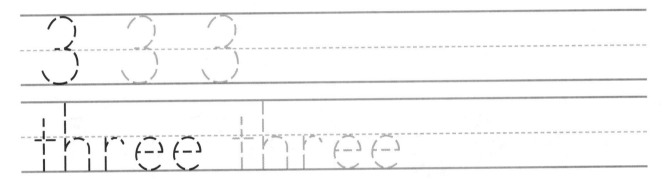

Directions: Color the cows. Practice writing the numeral and number word.

four cows

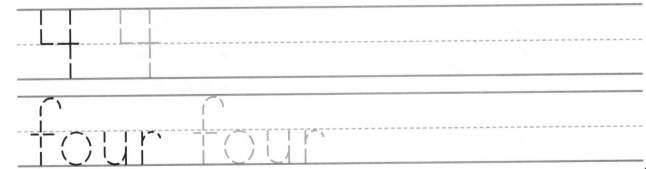

MATH

Skill 5: Counting 0 Through 4

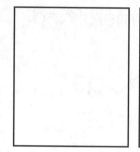    

zero	one	two	three	four
0	I	2	3	4

Directions: Circle the number.

0   I   2   (3)   4

0   I   2   3   4

0   I   2   3   4

0   I   2   3   4

0   I   2   3   4

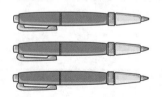

0   I   2   3   4

14

100 Kindergarten Skills

Skill 5: Counting 0 Through 4

Directions: Monsters like to blow bubbles! Draw more bubbles to make a total of **4** in each row. To prove your work, write the numbers **1**, **2**, **3**, and **4** on the bubbles in each row.

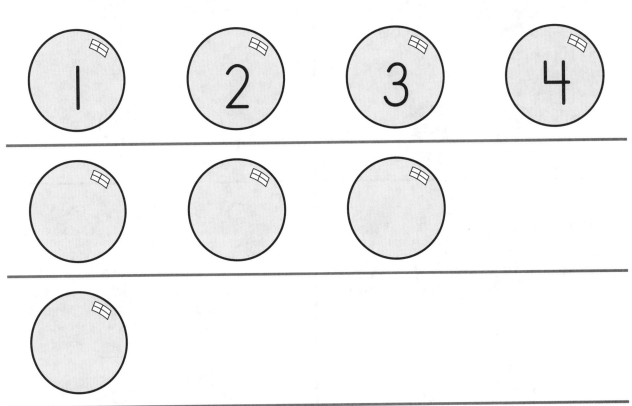

Directions: Learn a rhyme: "One for the monster, two for the show, three to get ready, and four to go." Hold up 1 finger, then 2, then 3, then 4.

MATH

Directions: Count the number of objects out loud. Then, color the correct number.

3   **5**

2   3

4   3

4   5

3   4

2   5

6: Counting 0 Through 5

Directions: Count each set of objects. Circle the correct number.

   1 2 3 4 5

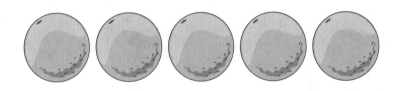   1 2 3 4 5

            1 2 3 4 5

   1 2 3 4 5

   1 2 3 4 5

MATH

Directions: Circle the objects to make 5. Trace the number. Write the number.

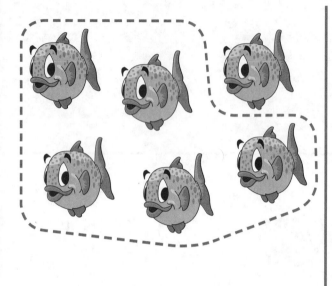

5

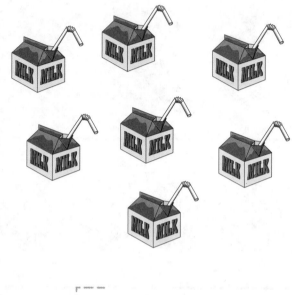

Directions: Color the boats. Practice writing the numeral and number word.

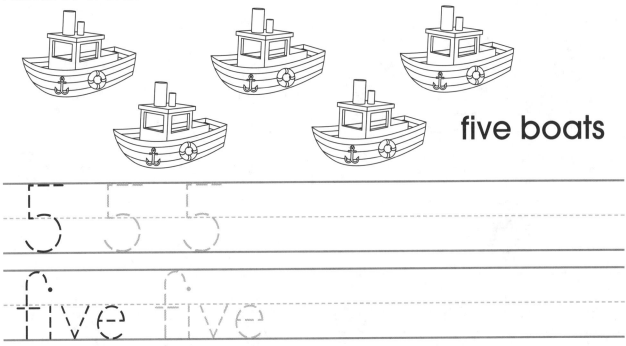

five boats

5 5 5

five five five

Directions: Circle and color five fish.

8: Counting 6 and 7

Directions: Count the number of objects out loud. Then, color the correct number.

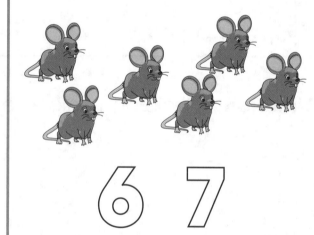

Directions: Circle and color six coats.

Directions: Circle and color seven birds.

MATH

Directions: Count the number of objects in each group out loud. Trace the number. Write the number.

6   **6**

_____   _____

7   **7**

_____   _____

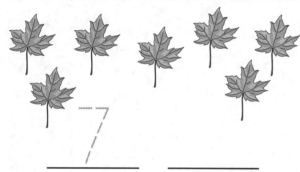

7

_____   _____

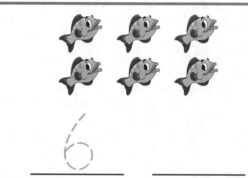

6

_____   _____

6

_____   _____

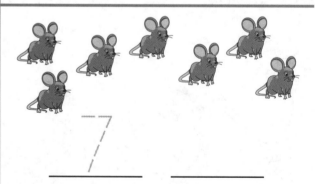

7

_____   _____

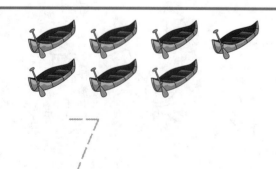

7

_____   _____

6

_____   _____

Skill 9: Writing 6 and 7

Directions: Color the igloos. Practice writing the numeral and number word.

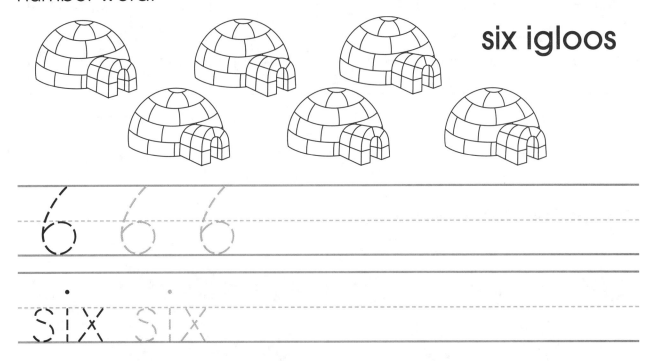

six igloos

6   6   6

six six

Directions: Color the nests. Practice writing the numeral and number word.

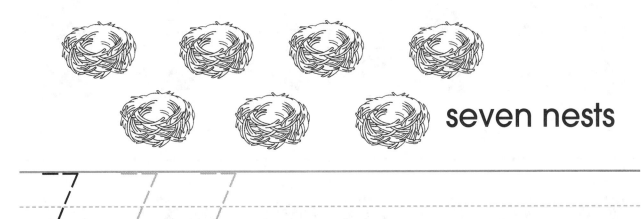

seven nests

7   7   7

seven seven

MATH

Skill 10: Counting 5 Through 7

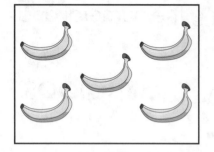

five
5

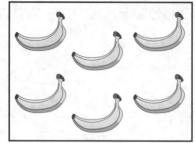

six
6

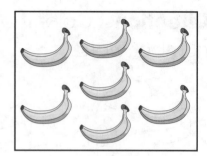

seven
7

Directions: Circle the number.

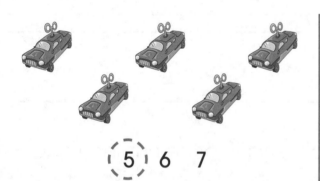

(5) 6 7

5 6 7

5 6 7

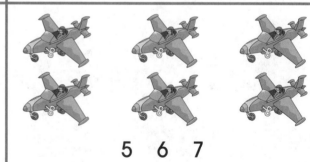

5 6 7

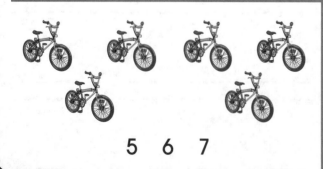

5 6 7

5 6 7

MATH

24

100 Kindergarten Skills

10: Counting 5 Through 7

Directions: Count each set of objects. Circle the correct number.

5   6   7

5   6   7

5   6   7

5   6   7

5   6   7

5   6   7

MATH

Skill 11: Counting 8 and 9

Directions: Circle the objects to make the given number. Then, color the number.

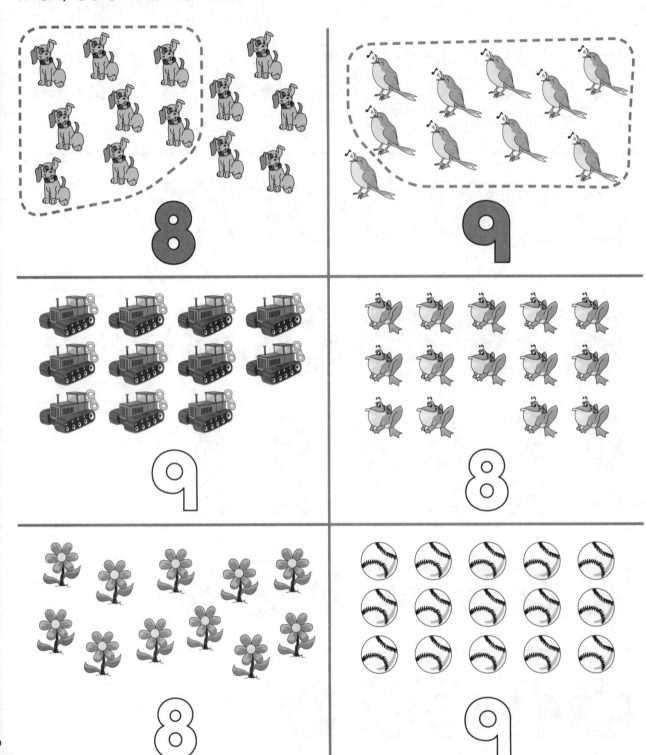

Directions: Circle and color eight spiders.

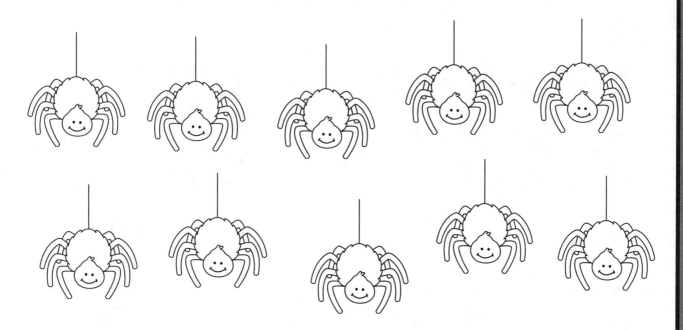

Directions: Circle and color nine horses.

Directions: Count the number of objects in each group out loud. Trace the number. Write the number.

8

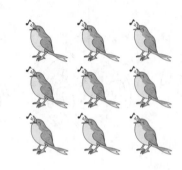

9

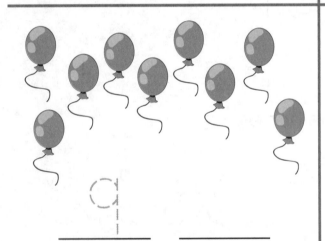

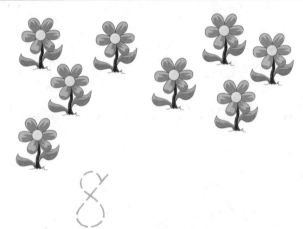

12 : Writing 8 and 9

Directions: Color the webs. Practice writing the numeral and number word.

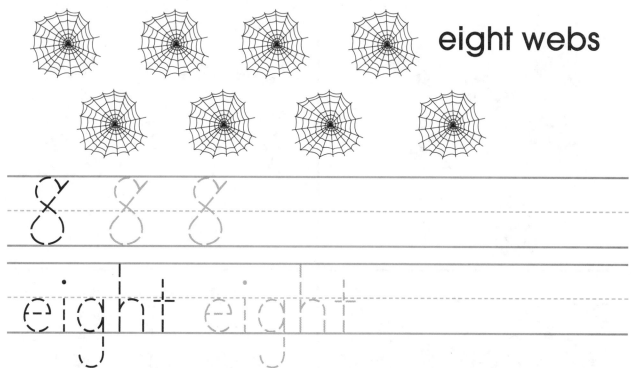

eight webs

8 8 8

eight eight

Directions: Color the hats. Practice writing the numeral and number word.

nine hats

9 9 9

nine nine

MATH

Directions: Count the number of objects in each group out loud. Then, color the correct number.

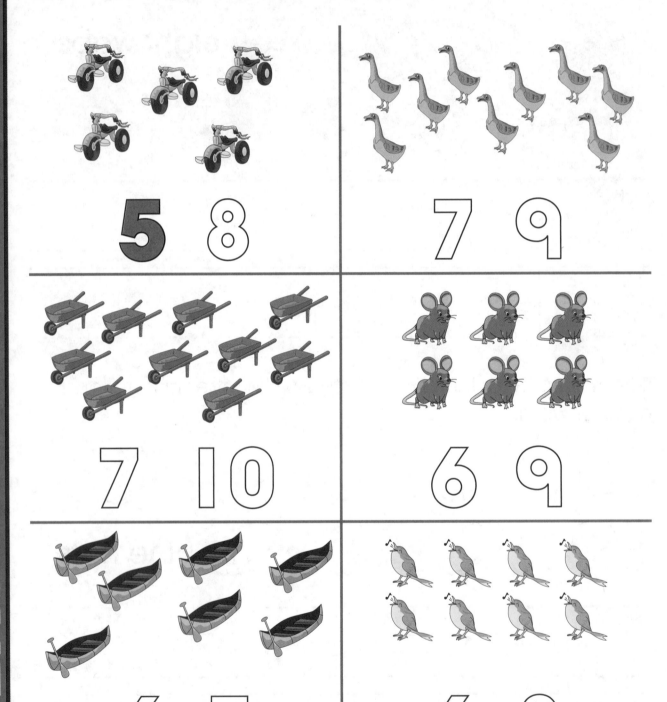

Directions: Draw a line to match each set of drawers to the correct set of shirts.

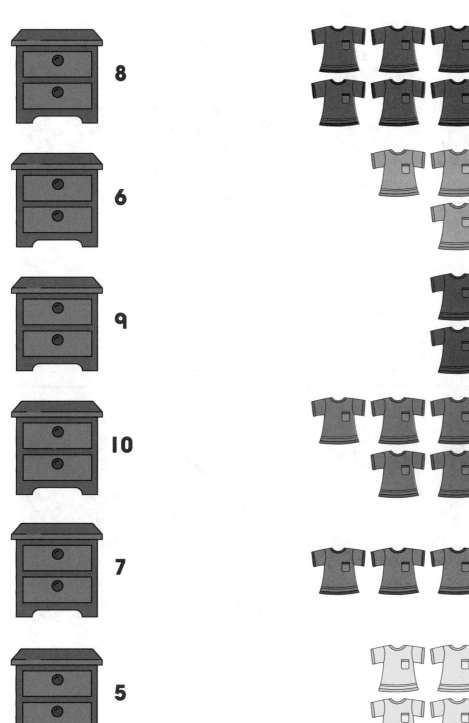

8

6

9

10

7

5

MATH

Directions: Cross out the extra objects in each group to make 10. Trace the number. Write the number.

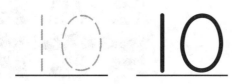 

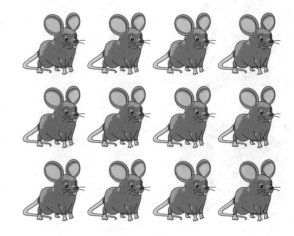

MATH

Directions: Color the bats. Practice writing the numeral and number word.

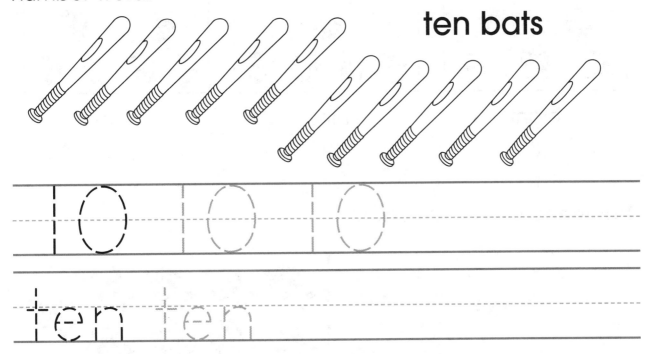

ten bats

Directions: Circle and color ten balls.

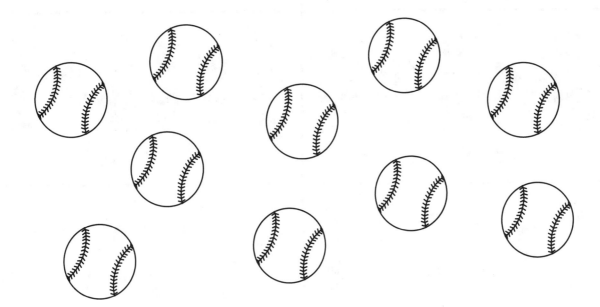

MATH

eight	nine	ten
8	9	10

Directions: Circle the number.

8 (9) 10

8   9   10

8   9   10

8   9   10

8   9   10

Skill 15: Counting 8 Through 10

Directions: Count the number of objects in each row. Circle the correct numeral.

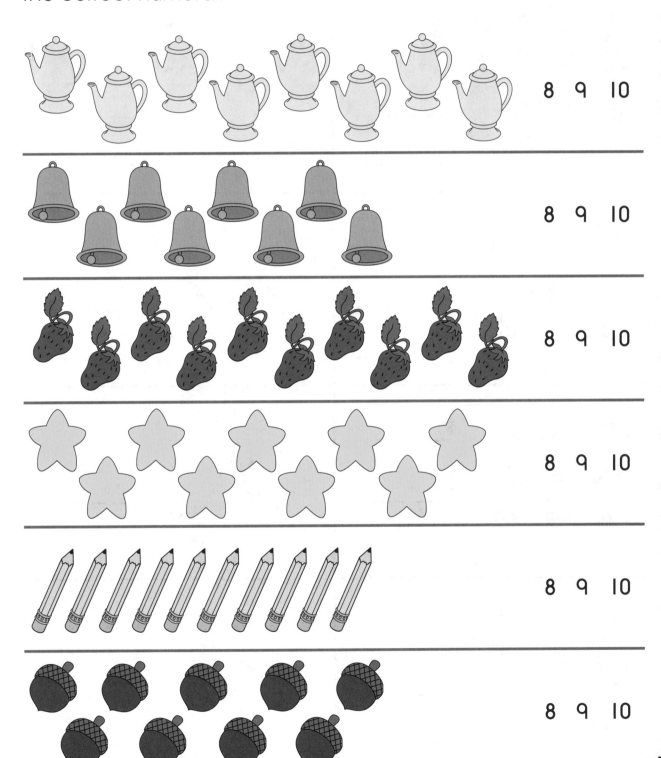

8   9   10

8   9   10

8   9   10

8   9   10

8   9   10

8   9   10

MATH

Skill 16: Counting and Writing 0 Through 10

Directions: Count how many. Write the number.

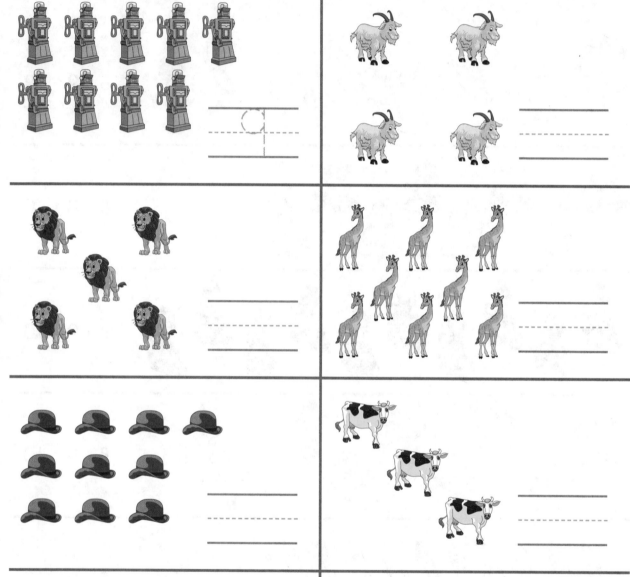

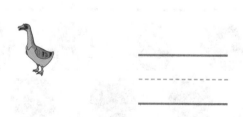

MATH

Skill 16: Counting and Writing 0 Through 10

Directions: Count how many. Write the number.

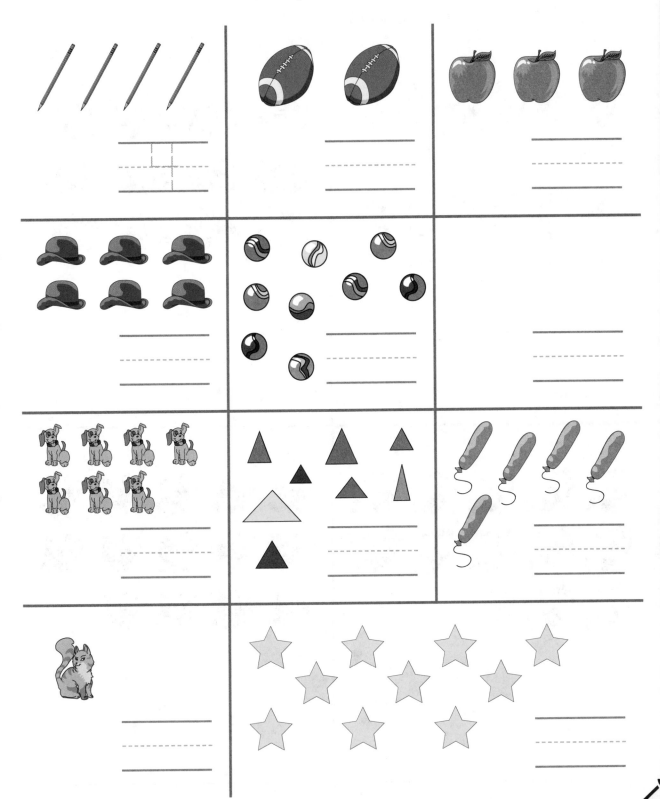

Directions: Count the objects in each group out loud. Trace the number. Write the number.

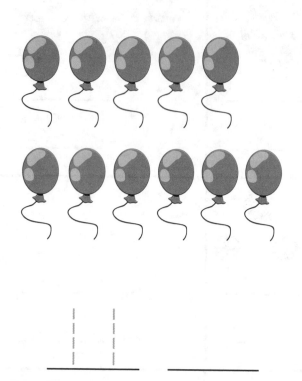

11

12

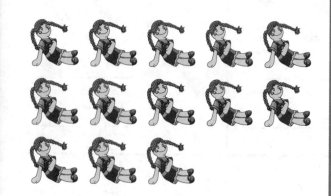

13

14

Directions: Draw a line to connect the number with the matching set of monsters.

11

13

12

11

12

14

13

MATH

18: Counting 15 Through 18

Directions: Count the objects in each group out loud. Trace the number. Write the number.

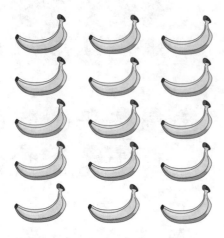

1 5 ___ ___

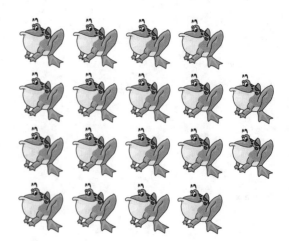

1 6 ___ ___

1 7 ___ ___

1 8 ___ ___

Directions: Count the number of objects in each row. Circle the correct numeral.

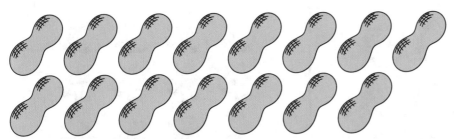

15   16   17   18

15   16   17   18

15   16   17   18

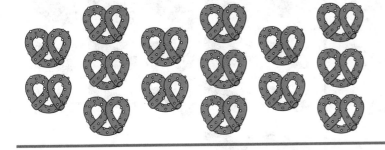

15   16   17   18

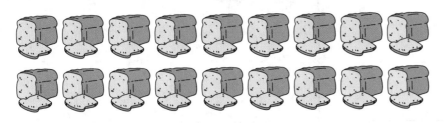

15   16   17   18

19: Counting 19 Through 22

Directions: Count the objects in each group out loud. Trace the number. Write the number.

19 _____

20 _____

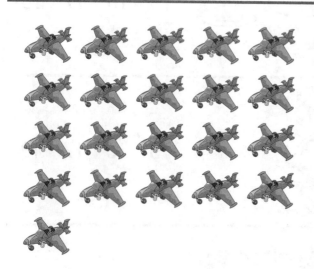

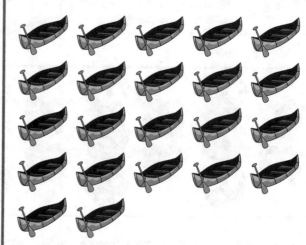

21 _____

22 _____

Directions: Count each set of fruit. Circle the correct number.

19   22

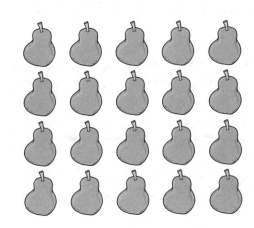

20   22

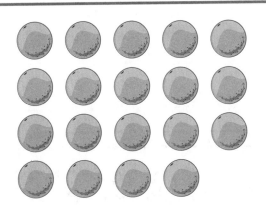

18   19

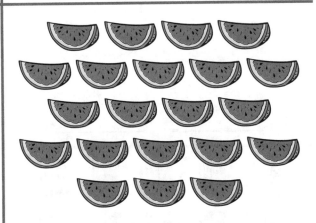

19   21

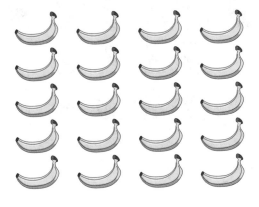

20   21

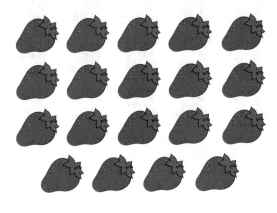

17   19

MATH

Directions: Count the objects in each group out loud. Trace the number. Write the number.

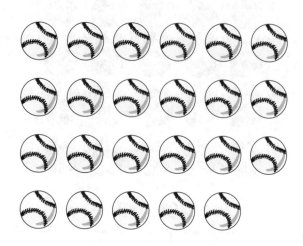

23 _____ _____

24 _____ _____

25 _____ _____

26 _____ _____

Directions: Draw the correct number of items in each box.

23 apples	24 flowers
25 frogs	26 balloons

Skill **21**: Counting 27 Through 30

Directions: Count the objects in each group out loud. Trace the number. Write the number.

27 _____

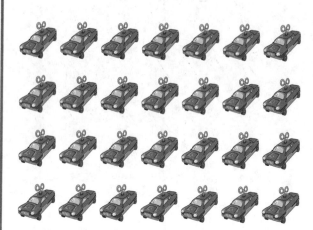

28 _____

2̲9̲ _____

30 _____

MATH

46

Directions: Count each set. Write the correct number in each box.

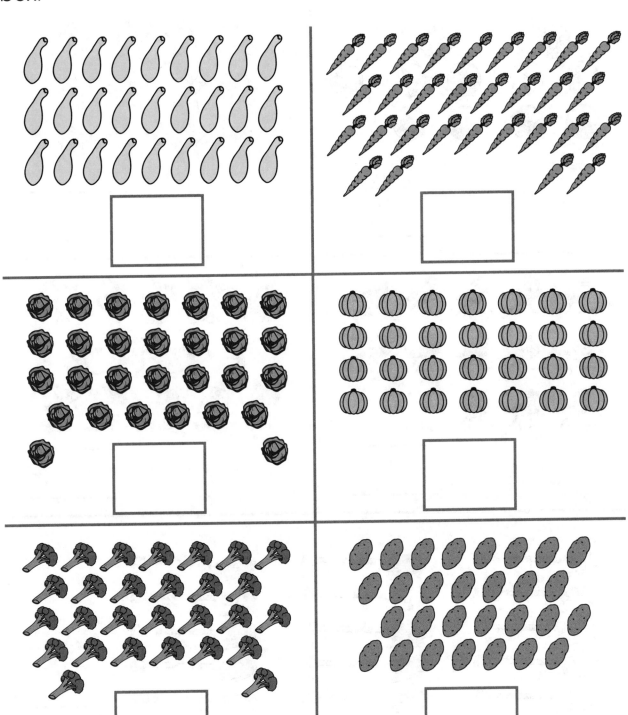

22: Counting and Writing
11 Through 20

Directions: Count how many. Trace the number.

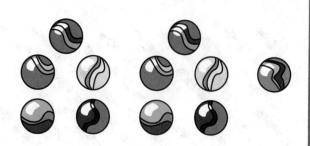

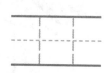

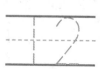

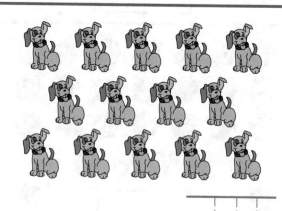

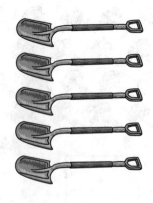

Skill 22: Counting and Writing 11 Through 20

Directions: Count how many. Trace the number.

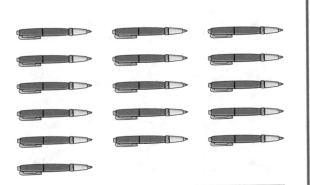

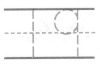

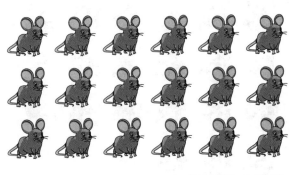

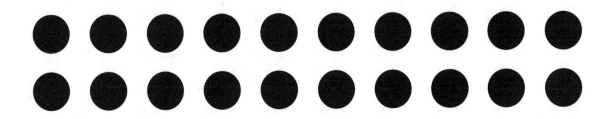

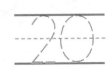

MATH

23: Counting and Writing 21 Through 30

Directions: Count how many. Trace the number.

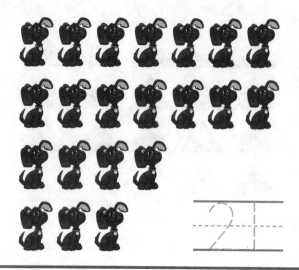

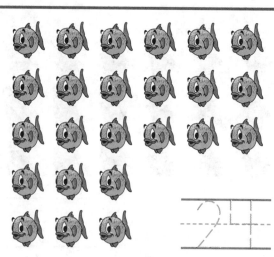

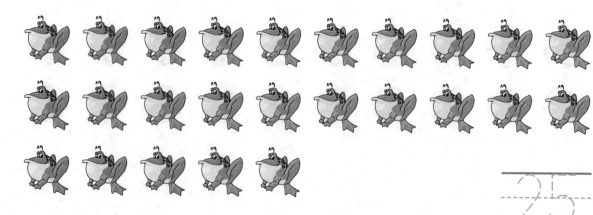

23: Counting and Writing
21 Through 30

Directions: Count how many. Trace the number.

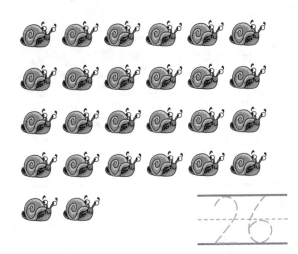

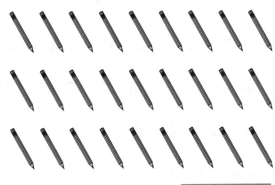

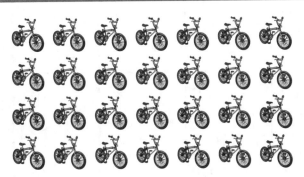

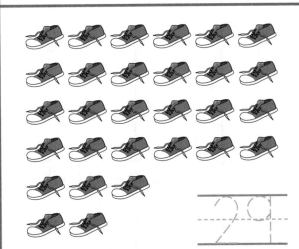

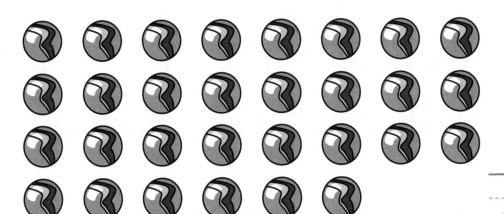

MATH

Directions:

1. Circle the name of the month.

2. Draw a box around the days of the week.

3. Color the first day of the month red.

4. Color the last day of the month blue.

MARCH						
SUNDAY	MONDAY	TUESDAY	WEDNESDAY	THURSDAY	FRIDAY	SATURDAY
	1	2	3	4	5	6
7	8	9	10	11	12	13
14	15	16	17	18	19	20
21	22	23	24	25	26	27
28	29	30	31			

Directions: Write how many days are in this month. _____

Skill 24: Reading a Calendar

Directions: Trace and say the name of the month July. Say the names of the days of the week. Trace and then write the numbers to complete the calendar.

JULY

SUNDAY	MONDAY	TUESDAY	WEDNESDAY	THURSDAY	FRIDAY	SATURDAY
				1	2	3
		6	7			10
11			14		16	
	19				23	
25						31

MATH

Skill 25: Counting to 100

Directions: Count the number of objects out loud by ones and by tens. Trace the number. Write the number.

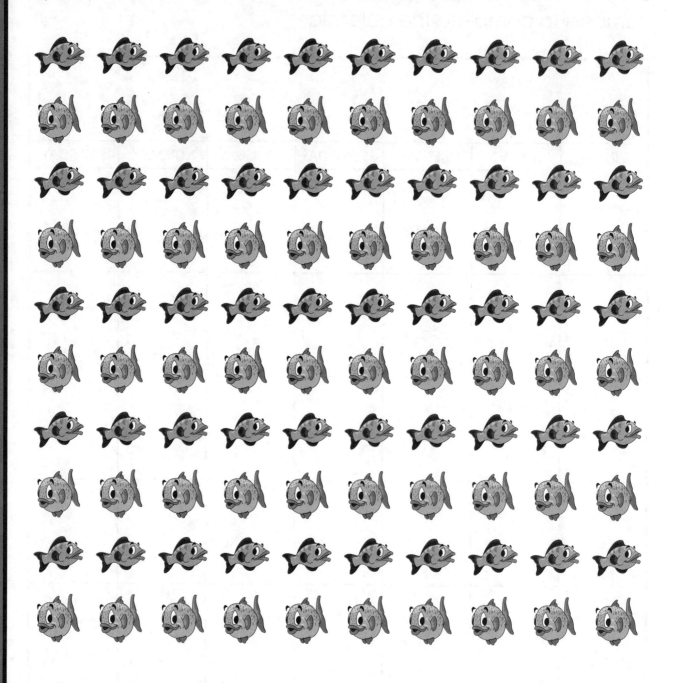

100

Skill 25: Counting to 100

Directions: Help the monkey find the bananas. Color the numbers in order from 10 to 100.

10 20 30 40 30 70 20 40 60 90 50 50 90 100 100 80 60 90 100 70 80 90 70 60

MATH

26: Comparing Numbers
0 Through 5

Directions: Circle the number that is greater.

5	3	3	1
2	4	1	2

Directions: Circle the number that is less.

5	1	4	1
3	4	5	2

26: Comparing Numbers
0 Through 5

Directions: Circle the number that is greater.

Directions: Circle the number that is less.

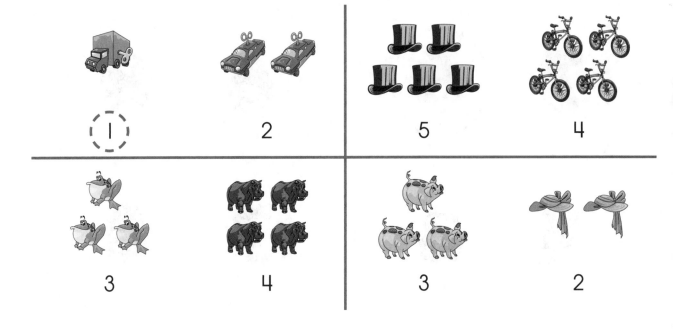

MATH

Skill 27: Comparing Numbers 6 Through 9

Directions: Circle the number that is greater.

6

9   7

6   9

7   8

Directions: Circle the number that is less.

7

6   8

9   8

7   8

Skill 27: Comparing Numbers 6 Through 9

Directions: Circle the number that is greater.

Lisa saw 9 .

Joe saw 7  .

Tanya saw 8 .

Dora saw 6 .

Jada saw 6 .

Alex saw 7 .

Chae saw 7 .

Tom saw 9  .

Directions: Circle the number that is less.

Dede saw 7 .

Juan saw 6 .

Aleta saw 8 .

Carl saw 9 .

Brent saw 9 .

Kida saw 6 .

Lili saw 9  .

Abby saw 8 .

MATH

Skill 28: Adding More (Addition)

Directions: Two kittens are joined by one more kitten. Count the total number of kittens. Trace the number that shows how many kittens there are now.

$$3$$

Directions: There are 3 fish in a pond and 1 more fish joins them. Count the number of fish altogether. Trace the number that shows the number of fish.

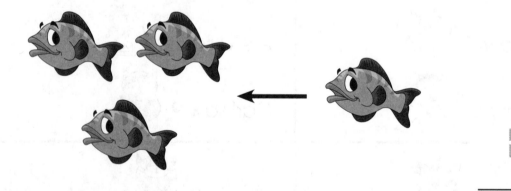

$$4$$

Skill 28: Adding More (Addition)

Directions: Read the story problems. Write the number sentences.

Daniel picked 2 pumpkins. Sam picked 3 pumpkins. How many pumpkins did the boys pick altogether?

_____ + _____ = _____

The boys picked _____ pumpkins altogether.

Katie blew up 1 balloon. Claire blew up 3 balloons. How many balloons did the girls blow up altogether?

_____ + _____ = _____

The girls blew up _____ balloons altogether.

Max and his brother helped their dad decorate tables for the party. They decorated 2 tables. How many tables were decorated altogether?

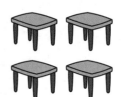

_____ + _____ = _____

The boys decorated _____ tables altogether.

MATH

29: Taking Away (Subtraction)

Directions: There are 3 birds in a tree. One flies away. Count the number of birds that are left. Trace the number that shows how many birds are left.

2

Directions: There are 4 baseball caps hanging on a hat rack. One cap is taken away. Count the number of caps that are left. Trace the number that shows how many caps are left.

3

Skill 29: Taking Away (Subtraction)

Directions: Read the story problems. Write the number sentences.

Parker hit 3 baseballs. Two of them were home runs and went out of the park. How many baseballs were not hit out of the park?

_____ – _____ = _____

There was _____ baseball not hit out of the park.

Four players are on one team. Two of them are in the dugout. The rest are on the field. How many players are on the field?

_____ – _____ = _____

There are _____ players on the field.

Molly's team had 5 baseball gloves. They gave 3 of them to the other team. How many baseball gloves does Molly's team have left?

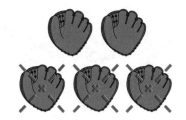

_____ – _____ = _____

Molly's team has _____ baseball gloves left.

MATH

Skill 30: Adding Through 3

Directions: Count the total number of objects in each section. Write the number on the line.

$$\begin{array}{r} 1 \\ + 1 \\ \hline 2 \end{array}$$

$$\begin{array}{r} 2 \\ + 1 \\ \hline \end{array}$$

$$\begin{array}{r} 1 \\ + 2 \\ \hline \end{array}$$

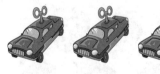

$$\begin{array}{r} 3 \\ + 0 \\ \hline \end{array}$$

$$\begin{array}{r} 0 \\ + 3 \\ \hline \end{array}$$

30: Adding Through 3

Directions: Count the total number of objects in each section.
Write the number on the line.

$$\begin{array}{r} 2 \\ + 1 \\ \hline 3 \end{array}$$

$$\begin{array}{r} 3 \\ + 0 \\ \hline \end{array}$$

$$\begin{array}{r} 1 \\ + 2 \\ \hline \end{array}$$

$$\begin{array}{r} 1 \\ + 1 \\ \hline \end{array}$$

$$\begin{array}{r} 1 \\ + 0 \\ \hline \end{array}$$

MATH

Directions: Count the number of objects left after the crossed out objects are removed. Write the number of remaining objects on the line.

$$\begin{array}{r} 3 \\ -1 \\ \hline 2 \end{array}$$

$$\begin{array}{r} 3 \\ -0 \\ \hline \end{array}$$

$$\begin{array}{r} 2 \\ -1 \\ \hline \end{array}$$

$$\begin{array}{r} 3 \\ -2 \\ \hline \end{array}$$

$$\begin{array}{r} 1 \\ -1 \\ \hline \end{array}$$

Skill 31: Subtracting Through 3

Directions: Subtract.

There are 3 apples on a tree. One falls off. How many apples are left?	There are 2 markers on a table. Jill loses 1. How many markers are left?
There are 3 pairs of scissors in our room. We gave 2 to another class. How many are left?	Ms. Morio has 1 apple on her desk. She eats it. How many apples are left?
Lee has 2 pencils. José borrows 1. How many pencils does Lee have left?	There are 3 students outside. Two come inside. How many students are still outside?

MATH

Directions: Count the total number of objects in each section. Write the number on the line.

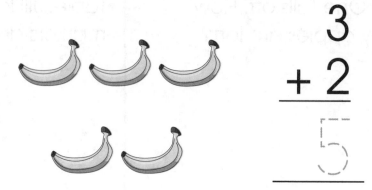

$$\begin{array}{r} 3 \\ + 2 \\ \hline 5 \end{array}$$

$$\begin{array}{r} 2 \\ + 3 \\ \hline \end{array}$$

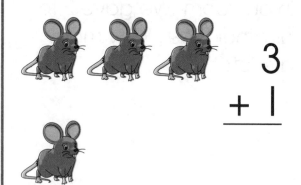

$$\begin{array}{r} 3 \\ + 1 \\ \hline \end{array}$$

$$\begin{array}{r} 1 \\ + 4 \\ \hline \end{array}$$

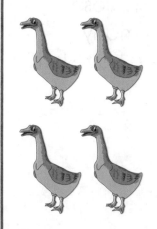

$$\begin{array}{r} 2 \\ + 2 \\ \hline \end{array}$$

Skill 32: Adding to 4 and 5

Directions: Add. Write the sums. Draw lines through the tunnels to connect each matching sum.

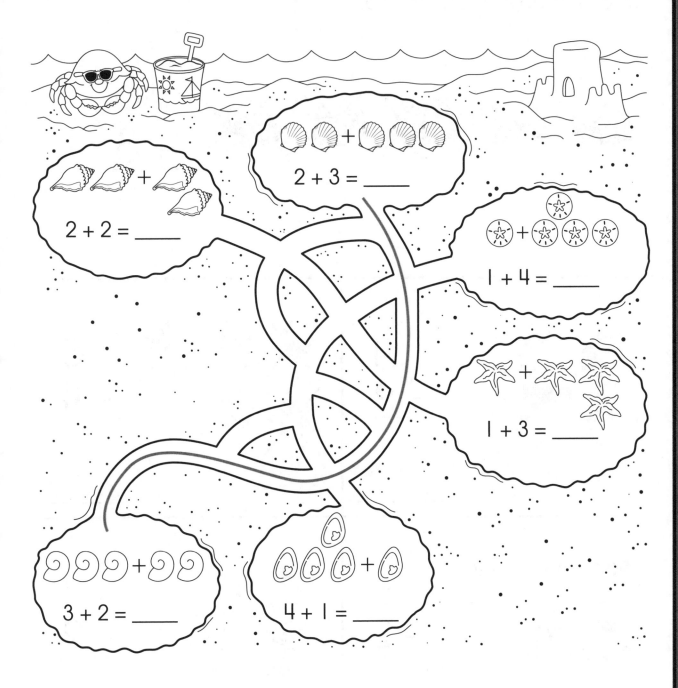

MATH

Directions: Count the number of objects left after the crossed out objects are removed. Write the number of remaining objects on the line.

$$\begin{array}{r} 5 \\ -\ 3 \\ \hline 2 \end{array}$$

$$\begin{array}{r} 4 \\ -\ 1 \\ \hline \end{array}$$

$$\begin{array}{r} 5 \\ -\ 4 \\ \hline \end{array}$$

$$\begin{array}{r} 5 \\ -\ 2 \\ \hline \end{array}$$

$$\begin{array}{r} 4 \\ -\ 2 \\ \hline \end{array}$$

Skill 33: Subtracting From 4 and 5

Directions: Subtract. Write the number sentences.

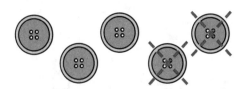

Cross out 2.
How many are left?

5 - 2 = 3

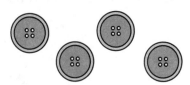

Cross out 1.
How many are left?

_____ - _____ = _____

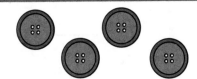

Cross out 3.
How many are left?

_____ - _____ = _____

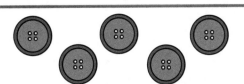

Cross out 0.
How many are left?

_____ - _____ = _____

Cross out 4.
How many are left?

_____ - _____ = _____

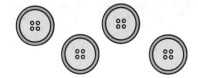

Cross out 2.
How many are left?

_____ - _____ = _____

Cross out 3.
How many are left?

_____ - _____ = _____

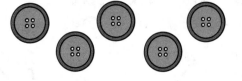

Cross out 5.
How many are left?

_____ - _____ = _____

MATH

SKILL 34: Adding to 6 and 7

Directions: Count the total number of objects in each section. Write the number on the line.

$$\begin{array}{r} 3 \\ + 4 \\ \hline 7 \end{array}$$

$$\begin{array}{r} 2 \\ + 5 \\ \hline \rule{1cm}{0.4pt} \end{array}$$

$$\begin{array}{r} 3 \\ + 3 \\ \hline \rule{1cm}{0.4pt} \end{array}$$

$$\begin{array}{r} 4 \\ + 2 \\ \hline \rule{1cm}{0.4pt} \end{array}$$

$$\begin{array}{r} 4 \\ + 3 \\ \hline \rule{1cm}{0.4pt} \end{array}$$

Directions: Solve each problem.

$5 + 1 =$ _____ $4 + 3 =$ _____ $3 + 3 =$ _____

$6 + 1 =$ _____ $3 + 4 =$ _____ $4 + 2 =$ _____

$1 + 5 =$ _____ $4 + 2 =$ _____ $0 + 7 =$ _____

Directions: Count the number of objects left after the crossed out objects are removed. Write the number of remaining objects on the line.

$$7$$
$$-\ 3$$
$$\underline{}$$
4

$$6$$
$$-\ 3$$
_____

$$7$$
$$-\ 2$$
_____

$$7$$
$$-\ 6$$
_____

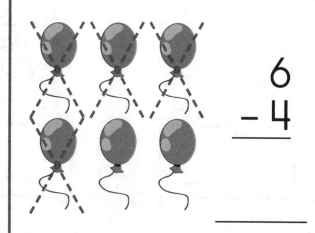

$$6$$
$$-\ 4$$
_____

Directions: Subtract. To help you subtract, cross out items in each backpack.

6 – 5 = _____

7 – 3 = _____

6 – 4 = _____

7 – 2 = _____

7 – 7 = _____

6 – 2 = _____

6 – 1 = _____

6 – 3 = _____

7 – 6 = _____

7 – 4 = _____

6 – 6 = _____

7 – 5 = _____

MATH

36: Adding to 8 and 9

Directions: Count the total number of objects in each section. Write the number on the line.

$$\begin{array}{r} 5 \\ + 3 \\ \hline 8 \end{array}$$

$$\begin{array}{r} 7 \\ + 1 \\ \hline \rule{2em}{0.4pt} \end{array}$$

$$\begin{array}{r} 6 \\ + 2 \\ \hline \rule{2em}{0.4pt} \end{array}$$

$$\begin{array}{r} 3 \\ + 6 \\ \hline \rule{2em}{0.4pt} \end{array}$$

$$\begin{array}{r} 4 \\ + 5 \\ \hline \rule{2em}{0.4pt} \end{array}$$

Skill 36: Adding to 8 and 9

Directions: Solve each problem. Draw a line from a frog that has the correct answer to the correct lily pad.

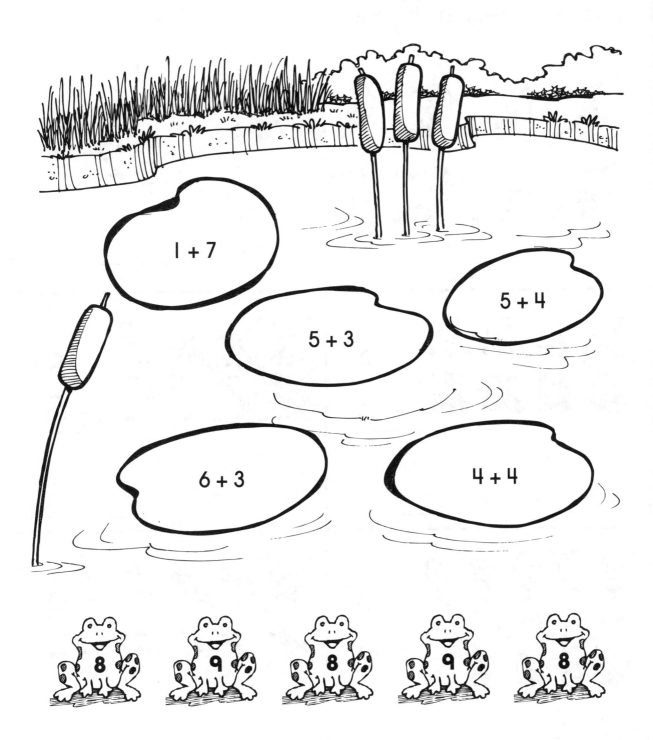

MATH

Directions: Count the number of objects left after the crossed out objects are removed. Write the number of remaining objects on the line.

9
– 2

_7_

8
– 3

_____

8
– 5

_____

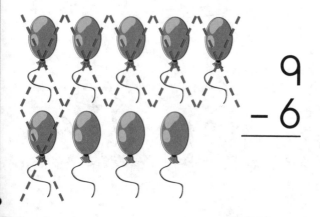

9
– 6

_____

9
– 4

_____

MATH

Directions: Write a subtraction problem to match each picture. Then find the difference.

____ - ____ = ____   ____ - ____ = ____   ____ - ____ = ____

____ - ____ = ____   ____ - ____ = ____   ____ - ____ = ____

____ - ____ = ____   ____ - ____ = ____   ____ - ____ = ____

____ - ____ = ____   ____ - ____ = ____   ____ - ____ = ____

MATH

Directions: Count the total number of objects in each section. Circle the number that makes 10.

$6 +$ _____ $= 10$

$1 \quad 4 \quad 2$

$9 +$ _____ $= 10$

$4 \quad 7 \quad 1$

$8 +$ _____ $= 10$

$3 \quad 5 \quad 2$

_____ $+ 5 = 10$

$5 \quad 8 \quad 9$

_____ $+ 3 = 10$

$5 \quad 7 \quad 4$

MATH

Skill 38: Making 10

Directions: Count the number of each item. Draw more to make each picture show 10. Write the number.

_____

_____

_____

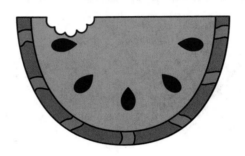

_____

_____

_____

MATH

Directions: Count the number of objects left after the crossed out objects are removed. Write the number of remaining objects on the line.

$$\begin{array}{r} 10 \\ -\ 4 \\ \hline 6 \end{array}$$

$$\begin{array}{r} 10 \\ -\ 7 \\ \hline \rule{1.5em}{0.4pt} \end{array}$$

$$\begin{array}{r} 10 \\ -\ 5 \\ \hline \rule{1.5em}{0.4pt} \end{array}$$

$$\begin{array}{r} 10 \\ -\ 2 \\ \hline \rule{1.5em}{0.4pt} \end{array}$$

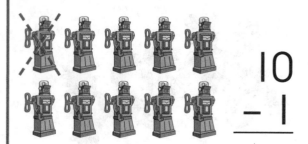

$$\begin{array}{r} 10 \\ -\ 1 \\ \hline \rule{1.5em}{0.4pt} \end{array}$$

Directions: Count the number of objects left after the crossed out objects are removed. Write the number of remaining objects on the line.

$10 - 3 = \underline{\hspace{2cm}}$

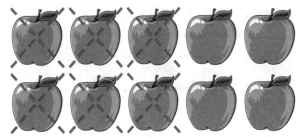

$10 - 6 = \underline{\hspace{2cm}}$

$10 - 8 = \underline{\hspace{2cm}}$

$10 - 9 = \underline{\hspace{2cm}}$

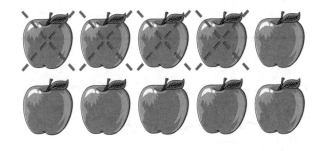

$10 - 4 = \underline{\hspace{2cm}}$

$10 - 0 = \underline{\hspace{2cm}}$

MATH

Directions: Color the **longer** picture blue. Color the **shorter** picture red.

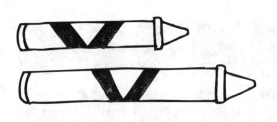

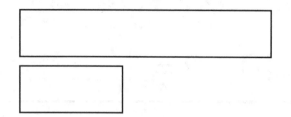
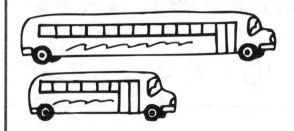

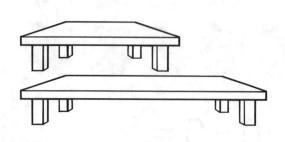
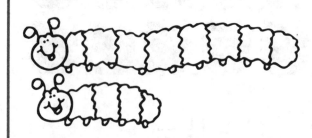

Skill **40**: Longer and Shorter

Directions: Color the **shorter** worm in each pair.

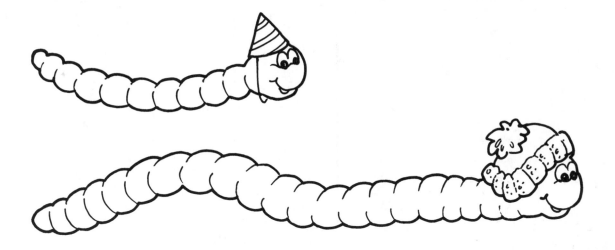

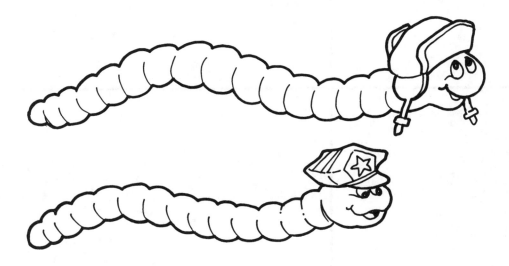

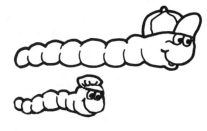

Directions: Color the **taller** object in each section green.
Color the **shorter** object yellow.

MATH

41: Taller and Shorter

Directions: Write a **T** on the **taller** house. Write an **S** on the **shorter** house.

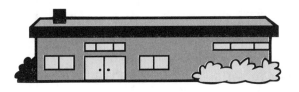

Directions: Circle the word that describes how each object compares to the bookshelf.

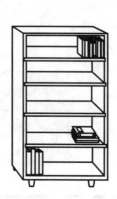

heavier   lighter   heavier   lighter

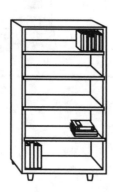
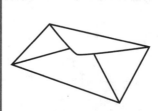

heavier   lighter   heavier   lighter

Skill **42**: Heavier and Lighter

Directions: Circle each correct answer.

Which object weighs less than the book on the scale?

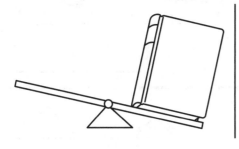   

Which object weighs more than the toy on the scale?

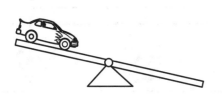   

Which object weighs about the same as the glue on the scale?

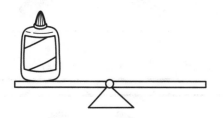  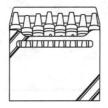 

Number the objects from lightest to heaviest. Write **1** for the lightest object. Write **3** for the heaviest object.

_____   _____   _____

MATH

Directions: How many? Write the number.

_____

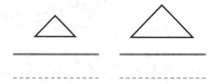

_____

_____

_____

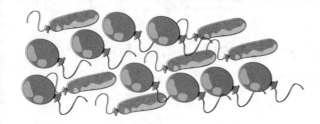

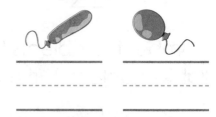

_____

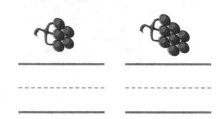

Skill 43: Sorting and Classifying Objects

Directions: Answer the questions.

How many birds? _____

How many lions? _____

How many animals with 4 legs? _____

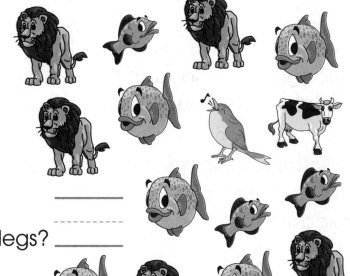

How many hats? _____

How many pairs of shoes? _____

How many pieces of fruit? _____

MATH

44: Identify Plane Shapes (2-D)

Shapes are named by the number of sides they have.

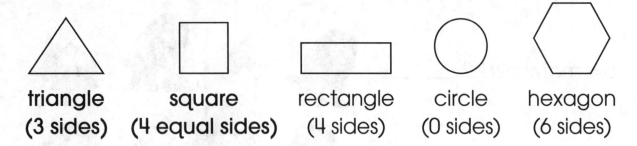

triangle
(3 sides)

square
(4 equal sides)

rectangle
(4 sides)

circle
(0 sides)

hexagon
(6 sides)

Directions: Color the triangles red. Color the squares orange. Color the rectangles yellow. Color the circles green. Color the hexagons blue.

Directions: Color the squares green. Color the rectangles yellow. Color the circles red. Color the triangles blue.

MATH

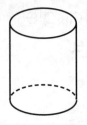
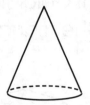
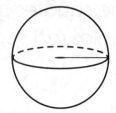
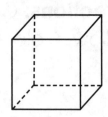

Color the **cylinders** blue.

Color the **cones** red.

Color the **spheres** green.

Color the **cubes** yellow.

SKILL 45: Identify Solid Shapes (3-D)

Directions: Use the code to color the figures.

 = red   = green   = blue   = orange

  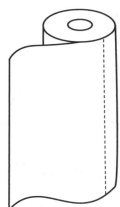 

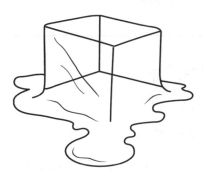  

How many ? _____   How many ? _____

How many 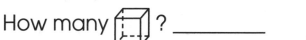 ? _____   How many ? _____

MATH

46: Squares

Directions: Color the square shapes green.

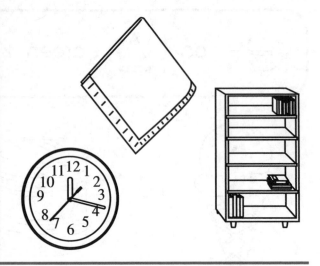

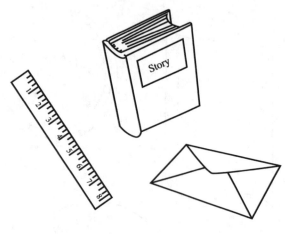

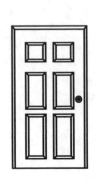

Skill 46: Squares

Directions: Look at all the shapes. Color the squares orange.

How many squares did you color? _____

Directions: Color the rectangle shapes yellow.

Directions: Look at all the shapes. Color the rectangles green.

MATH

Directions: Color the triangle shapes blue.

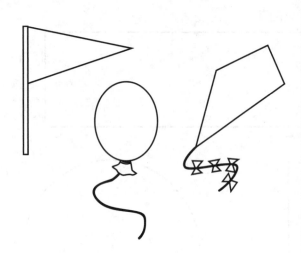
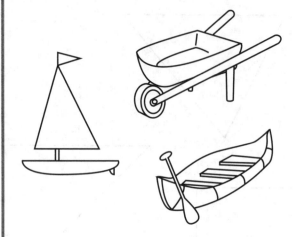
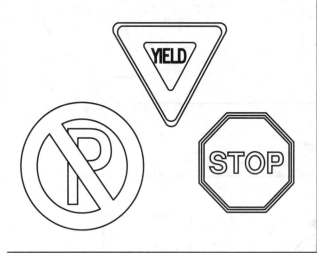
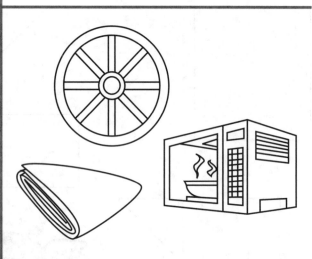

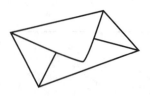

Skill **48**: Triangles

Directions: Look at all the shapes. Color the triangles red.

Skill 49: Circles

Directions: Color the circle shapes red.

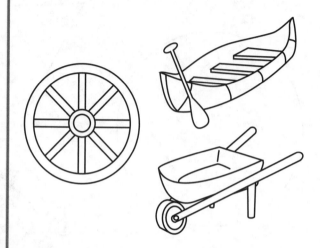

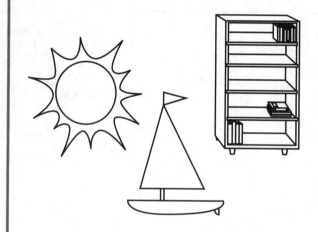

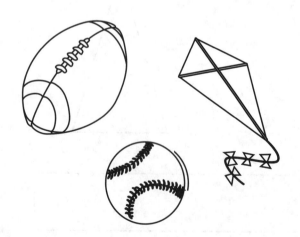

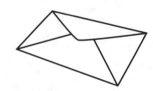

Directions: Look at all the shapes. Color the circles brown.

50: Finding and Composing Shapes

Directions: Color the triangles blue. Color the rectangles green. Color the circles yellow. Color the squares red.

Directions: Combine the following shapes. Trace the shape you get.

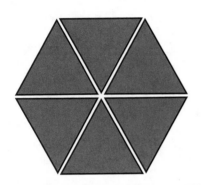 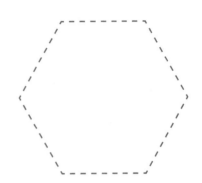

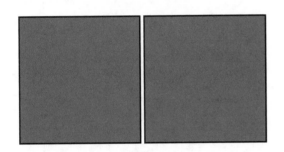 

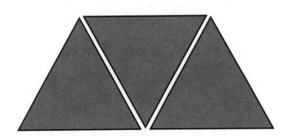 

 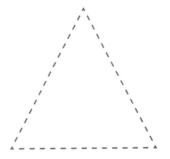

MATH

50 LANGUAGE ARTS SKILLS

Directions: Say each letter out loud.

Aa Bb Cc

Dd Ee Ff

Gg Hh Ii Jj

Kk Ll Mm

Nn Oo Pp

Qq Rr Ss Tt

Uu Vv Ww

Xx Yy Zz

Directions: Follow the letters in ABC order.

Skill 52: ABC Order

Directions: Follow the letters in ABC order to complete the house.

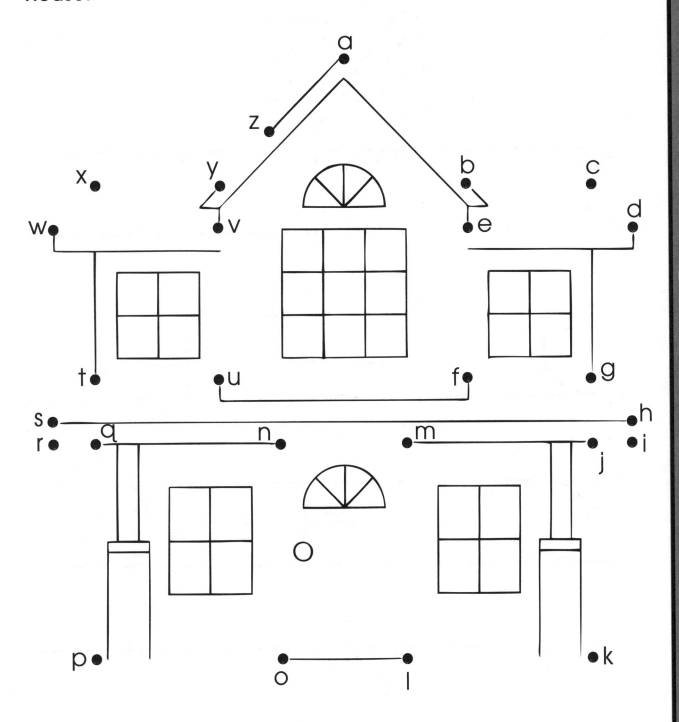

Directions: Trace the dotted lines to complete each **uppercase** letter.

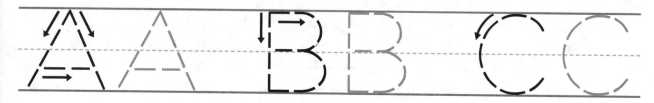

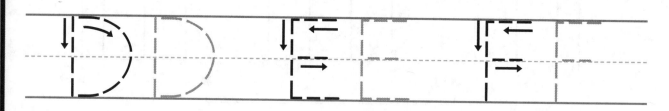

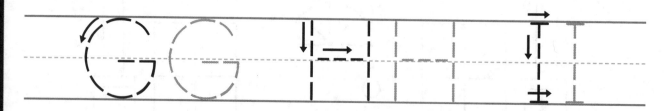

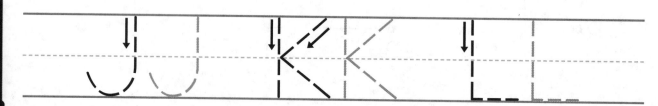

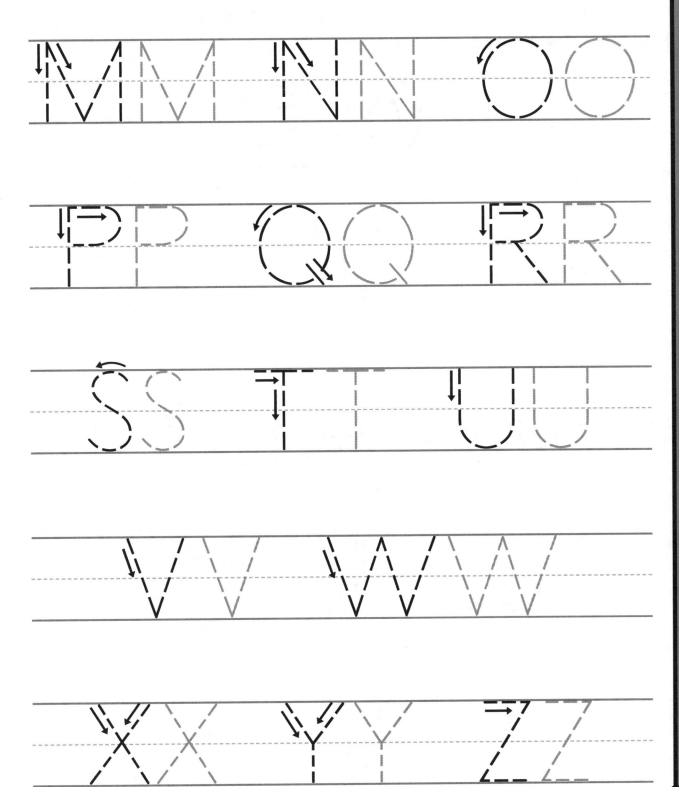

LANGUAGE ARTS

Directions: Trace the dotted lines to complete each **lowercase** letter.

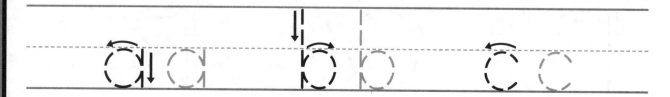

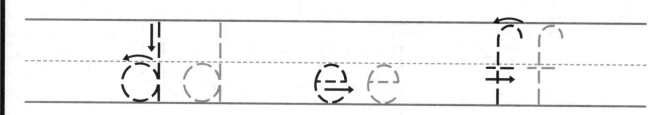

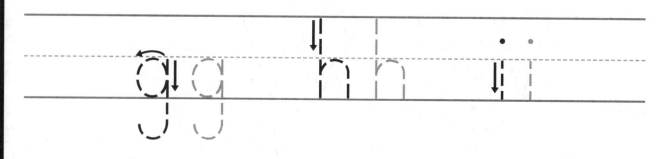

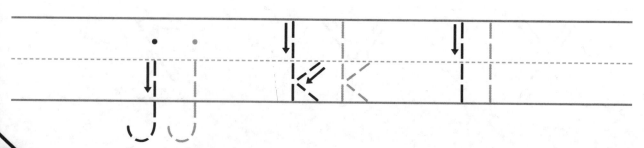

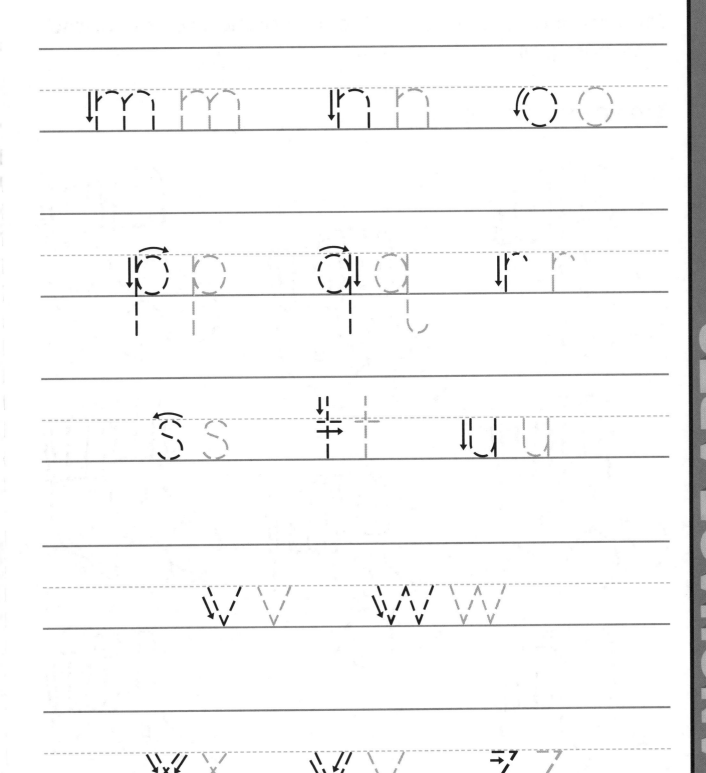

LANGUAGE ARTS

Directions: Color each pair of socks that shows a capital and lowercase pair.

Examples: **Zz   Jj**

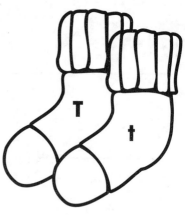

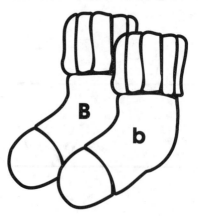

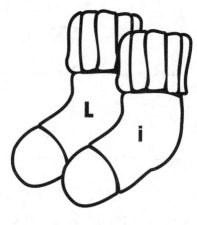

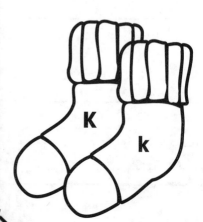

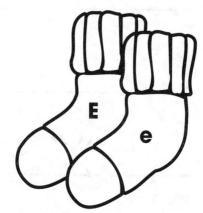

Directions: Draw a line to match each **capital** letter with the correct **lowercase** letter.

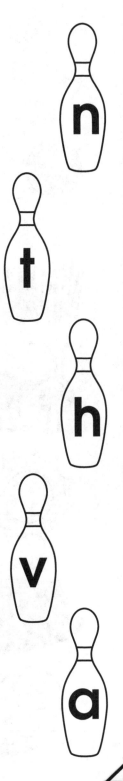

LANGUAGE ARTS

56: Letter Recognition

Directions: Name each picture. Circle the letter it starts with. Write the letter on the line.

	d	h	_____
	p	b	_____
	g	s	_____
	a	m	_____
	s	g	_____
	s	f	_____
	u	f	_____

LANGUAGE ARTS

Directions: Name each picture. Circle the words in each row that start with the same letter as the picture.

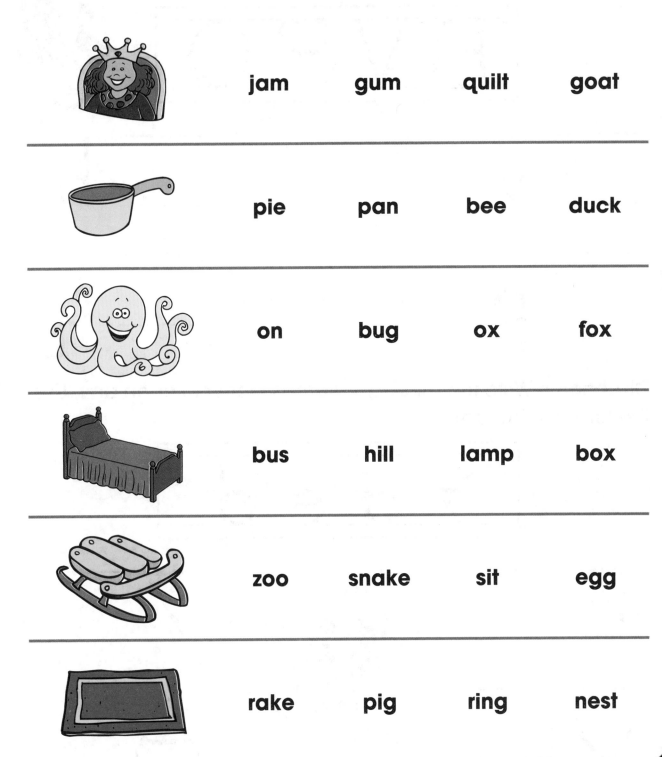

	jam	gum	quilt	goat
	pie	pan	bee	duck
	on	bug	ox	fox
	bus	hill	lamp	box
	zoo	snake	sit	egg
	rake	pig	ring	nest

LANGUAGE ARTS

Directions: Write the missing capital letter in each pair. Use the letters in the box.

v

b

p

q

Directions: Write the missing lowercase letter in each pair. Use the letters in the box.

E

Z

D

A

LANGUAGE ARTS

Directions: Say each picture name. Find the missing letter in the box. Write it on the line.

z h p f s u

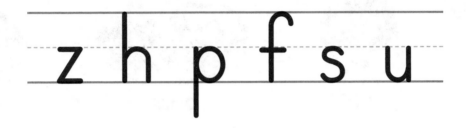

___ebra

___at

___lane

___ox

___ock

___mbrella

LANGUAGE ARTS

A **noun** is a naming word. It can name a person, place, or thing.

Examples:

girl   park   ball

Directions: Circle the **noun** that names each person.

        king   queen

        man   woman

        house   farmer

        baby   library

LANGUAGE ARTS

Skill 58: Common Nouns

Nouns can name things.

Examples:

boat

moon

Directions: Fill in the missing letters in the nouns that name things. Use the words in the box to help you.

book	desk	chair	bag	pen	apple

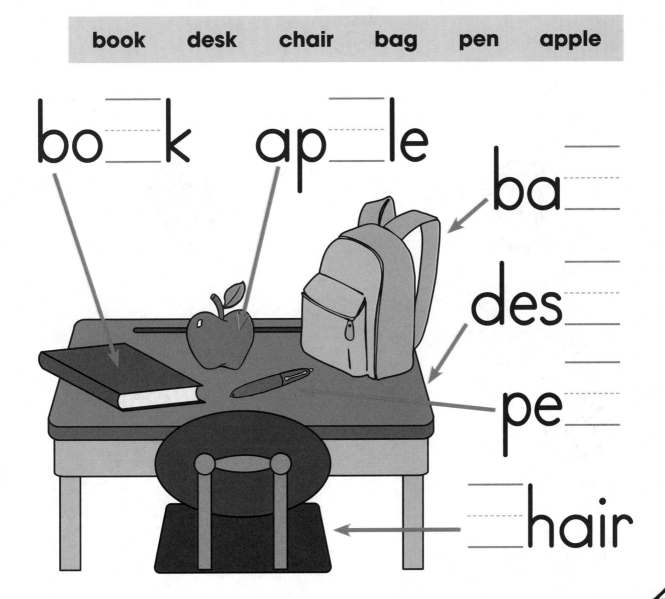

bo__k   ap__le

ba__

des__

pe__

__hair

LANGUAGE ARTS

Skill 59: Proper Nouns

A **proper noun** can name a certain person. Proper nouns start with capital letters.

Examples: **Dad**   **Grandpa**   **Andy**   **Jennifer**

Directions: Trace the names of the people in this family. Circle the capital letter in each name.

Skill 59: Proper Nouns

Directions: Each person or animal below has two names. Circle the name that is a proper noun. Make a line under the name that is a common noun.

Example: (Max) **boy**

Dan   firefighter

cat   Muffy

man   Grandpa

Annie   girl

A **verb** is an action word. It tells what happens in a sentence.

Examples: **jump** **laugh** **throw**

Directions: Anita and Tom are cooking. Circle the action word in each sentence that tells what they do.

Tom cuts.

Anita washes.

Anita mixes.

Anita stirs.

Tom peels.

They cook.

Directions: Name the action words below. Write the missing letters on the lines. Use the words in the box to help you.

| swim | dig | kick | eat | clap |

___at

cla___

di___

kic___

___wim

LANGUAGE ARTS

A **preposition** can show location (where) or time (when). Prepositions link nouns to other words in a sentence.

Examples: **on** the roof   **in** the cup

Directions: Trace the prepositions that match each picture.

in

under

beside

up

Skill 61: Prepositions

Directions: Choose a **preposition** to complete each sentence. Write it on the line.

to, on, with

Sam ran ______________ the park.

off, into, under

Rex hid ______________ the bed.

at, on, up

Sid's ball is ______________ the roof.

at, on, under

Mom will be home ______________ 6:00.

LANGUAGE ARTS

Skill 62: Pronouns

A **pronoun** can take the place of a person's name. **You**, **he**, **she**, **they**, and **it** are pronouns.

Example: Lola is seven.   **She** is seven.

Directions: Circle the pronoun in each sentence. Write it on the line.

He can skate.

_____

They make art.

_____

It is cold and windy.

_____

She likes to sing.

_____

You can color.

_____

Directions: Circle the pronoun to complete each sentence.
Use the pictures to help you.

He	She	**colors with green.**
She	It	**drives to work.**
She	They	**spill the paint!**
It	They	**is in the yard.**
She	It	**paints a picture.**
They	She	**helps clean**.

LANGUAGE ARTS

Skill 63: Sentences

A sentence is a group of words. It tells a complete thought. A sentence starts with a capital letter. It ends with a period.

Examples: **Len plays ball.**   **I like cats.**

Directions: Look at each sentence. Circle the capital letter. Circle the period.

A cat is by the tree.

Look at the moon.

It is cold.

I jump into bed.

I see stars.

I hear a bird.

There are no clouds.

Directions: Name each picture. Then, finish the sentence. Use the words in the box.

Soup	eyes	baby	sun	read	swim

_____

Mom likes to _____ .

_____

My sister is still a _____ .

_____

We like the _____ .

_____

My sister likes to _____ .

_____

_____ is our favorite dinner.

_____

Mom and I have brown _____ .

Skill **64**: Statements

A **statement** is a kind of sentence. A statement is a telling sentence. It starts with a capital letter. It ends with a period.

Directions: Look at each picture. Trace the statement. Circle the capital letter and the period. Write the statement on the line.

The beach is warm.

_____

- -

_____

I like winter.

_____

- -

_____

LANGUAGE ARTS

Skill 64: Statements

Directions: Look at each picture. Trace the statement. Circle the capital letter and the period. Write another telling sentence about the picture. Ask an adult to help you.

It is raining.

Kim likes autumn.

A **question** is a type of sentence. It is an asking sentence. It starts with a capital letter. It ends with a question mark.

Directions: Trace the question marks.

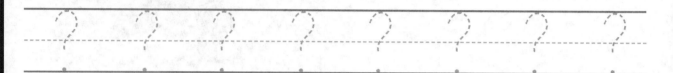

Directions: Add a question mark to the end of each question.

What do you see _____

Do you like cats _____

Do you have a pet _____

Where do you live _____

What is your favorite food _____

LANGUAGE ARTS

Skill **65**: Questions

Directions: Draw a line under each question. Circle the question mark.

Do you like to play ball?  **I play kickball.**

Do you swim?  **I love to swim.**

I draw animals.  **Can you draw?**

Do you skate?  **I skate at the park.**

When do they run?  **They run on Saturdays.**

LANGUAGE ARTS

Skill 66: Capitalizing the First Word in a Sentence

A **sentence** always starts with a capital letter.

Examples: (T)he cat is black.   (T)asha has two brothers.

Directions: Circle the capital letter that starts each sentence.

Tyler and Lin like to camp.

They need paint.

Will picks blue and green.

Bats fly like birds.

Where is the car?

Jen and Marco make a kite.

LANGUAGE ARTS

Directions: Each sentence should start with a capital letter. Write the word in the box on the line. Use a capital letter.

it	_____ is a windy day.
sam	_____ likes soccer.
he	_____ has a dog.
the	_____ kite takes off.
nico	_____ calls the cat.
he	_____ swims.
what	_____ a day we had!

LANGUAGE ARTS

Skill 67 : Capitalizing the Pronoun I

The word **I** is always spelled with a capital letter. It can start a sentence. It can be in the middle of a sentence.

Directions: Circle the word **I** in each sentence.

I like to hike.

Min and I went to camp.

I like apples.

I help him cook.

Dale and I told him what happened.

I asked Mom to drive us.

Dad and I love the woods.

LANGUAGE ARTS

Skill 67: Capitalizing the Pronoun I

Directions: The word **I** is missing from each sentence. Write a capital **I** on each line.

_____

_____ like to look for animals.

_____

Maria and _____ saw a bear once.

_____

_____ see lizards a lot.

_____

Mark and _____ want to see a snake.

_____

Will _____ see a deer one day?

_____

_____ hope so!

100 Kindergarten Skills

LANGUAGE ARTS

141

68: Capitalizing Names

Names start with a capital letter.

Examples: (A)ddy   (L)ex   (N)ora

Directions: Write your name on the line. Ask an adult if you need help.

_____

- -

_____

Directions: None of the names below start with a capital letter. Write each name on the line. Use a capital letter.

adam _____   **ivan** _____

lu _____   **pedro** _____

jackie _____   **amy** _____

luke _____   **heather** _____

The names of pets start with a capital letter, too.

Examples: Ⓛucky   Ⓐce

Directions: Each pet needs a name. Choose a name from the box. Write it under the pet. Use a capital letter.

bubbles	socks	spot	star	lily	bella	coco

_____

- - - - - - - - - - - - - - - - - - -

_____

_____

- - - - - - - - - - - - - - - - - - -

_____

_____

- - - - - - - - - - - - - - - - - - -

_____

_____

- - - - - - - - - - - - - - - - - - -

_____

LANGUAGE ARTS

Skill 69: Periods

A **period** comes at the end of a sentence. It shows you where the sentence ends.

Example: My cat's name is Daisy.

Directions: Circle the period in each sentence.

The rainbow is bright.

Pandas are cute.

Dogs can bark.

I hear bees buzz.

I lost my bike.

Grass is green.

Skill 69: Periods

Directions: Add a period to each sentence.

Bess has black hair _____

I need my umbrella _____

The zebra has stripes _____

Jaya has a green bag _____

Ben likes blue balloons _____

Yuri's jacket is yellow _____

A **question mark** comes at the end of a question. It shows you where the question ends.

Examples: Did you see the snake**(?)**   Why are you moving**(?)**

Directions: Circle each question mark.

Is lunch ready?

Do you like bananas?

Did you stir the soup?

Will Emma eat oranges?

Did you make salad?

Can we fry the eggs?

LANGUAGE ARTS

Skill 70: Question Marks

Directions: Write a question mark at the end of each question.

_____

Do you like cake _____

_____

Do you like baseball _____

_____

Was it windy _____

_____

Can we have pizza _____

_____

Are we out of juice _____

_____

What is a kiwi _____

Directions: Trace the letters and write them. Name each picture. Circle each picture whose name begins with the same sound as the first picture.

Directions: Trace the letters and write them. Name each picture. Circle each picture whose name begins with the same sound as the first picture.

Directions: Trace the letters and write them. Name each picture. Circle each picture whose name begins with the same sound as the first picture.

Directions: Trace the letters and write them. Name each picture. Circle each picture whose name begins with the same sound as the first picture.

LANGUAGE ARTS

Directions: Trace the letters and write them. Name each picture. Circle each picture whose name begins with the same sound as the first picture.

LANGUAGE ARTS

73: Sounds I, J, K, and L

Directions: Trace the letters and write them. Name each picture. Circle each picture whose name begins with the same sound as the first picture.

Directions: Trace the letters and write them. Name each picture. Circle each picture whose name begins with the same sound as the first picture.

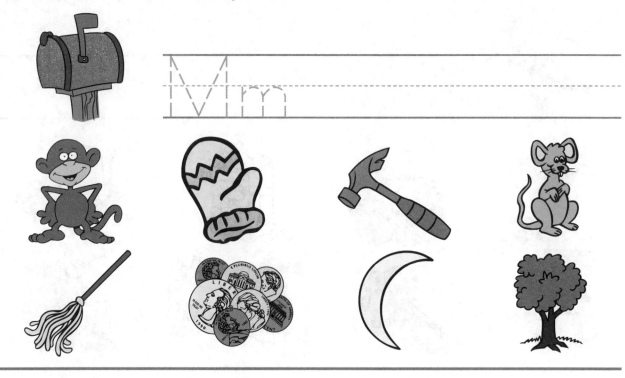

LANGUAGE ARTS

Directions: Trace the letters and write them. Name each picture. Circle each picture whose name begins with the same sound as the first picture.

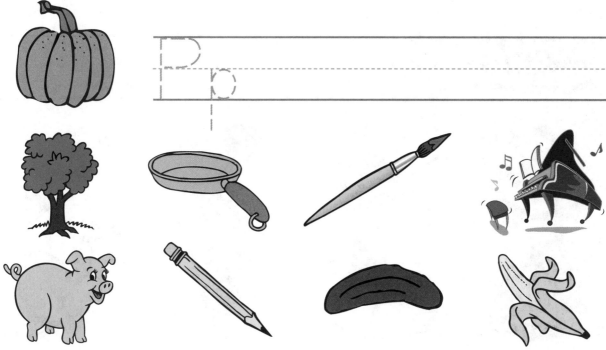

LANGUAGE ARTS

Directions: Trace the letters and write them. Name each picture. Circle each picture whose name begins with the same sound as the first picture.

LANGUAGE ARTS

Skill 75: Sounds Q, R, S, and T

Directions: Trace the letters and write them. Name each picture. Circle each picture whose name begins with the same sound as the first picture.

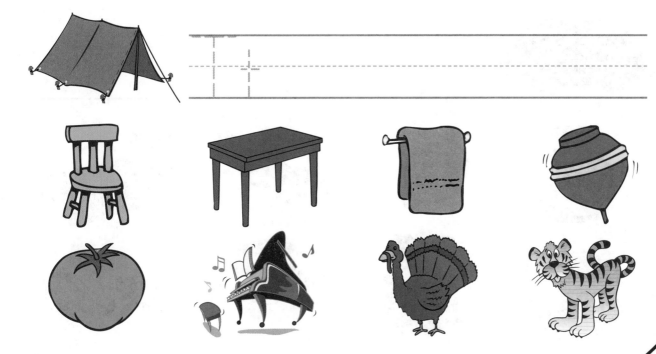

76: Sounds U, V, and W

Directions: Trace the letters and write them. Name each picture. Circle each picture whose name begins with the same sound as the first picture.

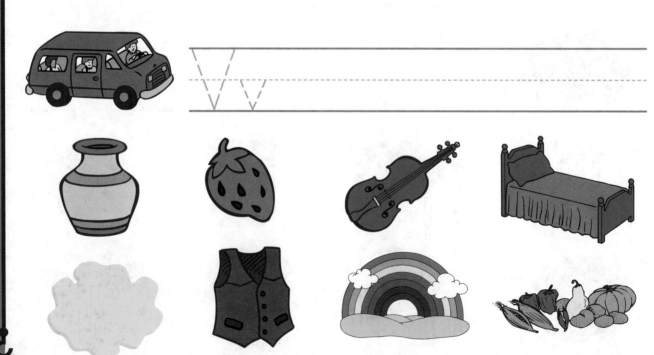

Directions: Trace the letters and write them. Name each picture. Circle each picture whose name begins with the same sound as the first picture.

Directions: Draw something that begins with each letter: **U, V,** and **W**.

Skill 77: Sounds: X, Y, and Z

Directions: Trace the letters and write them. Name each picture. Circle each picture whose name begins or ends with the same sound as the first picture.

Directions: Trace the letters and write them. Name each picture. Circle each picture whose name begins with the same sound as the first picture.

Directions: Draw something that begins with each letter: **X, Y,** and **Z.**

Directions: Say each picture name. Circle the letter for the beginning sound. Write the letter on the line.

g   d

_____

p   j

_____

l   b

_____

s   m

_____

m   d

_____

h   t

_____

LANGUAGE ARTS

Directions: Color the pictures in each row with the same beginning sound. Write the letter for the sound.

LANGUAGE ARTS

Skill 79: Ending Consonant Sounds

Directions: Circle the pictures in each row with the same ending sound. Write the letter for the sound.

_____

_____

_____

Skill 79: Ending Consonant Sounds

Directions: Say the name of each picture. Match the pictures that end with the same sound.

crab

net

web

pin

spoon

lid

lamp

bird

stamp

LANGUAGE ARTS

Short **a** makes the vowel sound you hear in **hat** .

Directions: Say the name of each picture. Circle the pictures that have the short **a** sound.

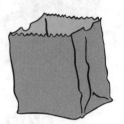

LANGUAGE ARTS

Directions: Color the pictures with a short **a** sound blue.

Short **e** makes the vowel sound you hear in **pen** .

Directions: Say the name of each picture. Fill in the missing letter for each word.

 w__b

 t__nt

 h__n

 sl__d

 b__ll

Directions: Color the fish with short **e** words green. Color the other fish yellow.

LANGUAGE ARTS

Skill 82: Short Vowel Sound i

Short **i** makes the vowel sound you hear in **wig** .

Directions: Help the fish find its pond. Follow the words that have the short **i** sound.

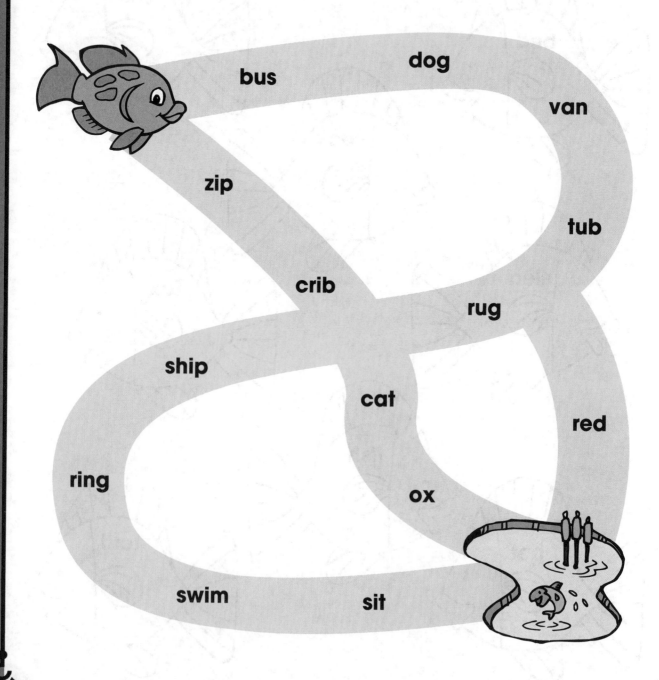

LANGUAGE ARTS

Skill 82: Short Vowel Sound i

Directions: Color the pictures with a short **i** sound green.

LANGUAGE ARTS

Short **o** makes the vowel sound you hear in **pot** .

Directions: Say the name of each picture. Circle the pictures that have the short **o** sound.

Directions: Color all the pictures with the short **o** sound blue.

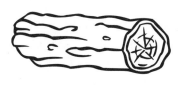  

LANGUAGE ARTS

Short **u** makes the vowel sound you hear in **brush** .

Directions: Say each picture name. Circle **u** if the vowel sound you hear in each word is the short **u** sound.

pumpkin  u

tub  u

umbrella u

cat  u

drum  u

dog u

LANGUAGE ARTS

84: Short Vowel Sound u

Directions: Say the name of each picture. Circle the pictures that have the short **u** sound.

LANGUAGE ARTS

Skill 85: Plural Nouns with s

Plural means **more than one**. Make a word plural by adding **s**.

Example: 1 goat  4 goats

Directions: Draw a line to match each word to the correct picture.

 **bats**

 **socks**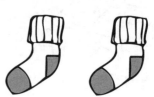

 **moon**

 **boats**

LANGUAGE ARTS

Directions: Look at each picture and word. If there is more than one of something, add **s**.

 sock__

 dress__

 hat__

 key__

 sun__

 coat__

LANGUAGE ARTS

A **prefix** is added to the beginning of a root word. It changes the word's meaning.

The prefix **un-** means **not**.   **Example: un**able = **not** able

The prefix **re-** means **again**.   **Example: re**play = play **again**

Directions: Circle the word that has a prefix in each sentence.

Jacob was unhappy with his sister.

Sam will reset the computer.

Can you retie the shoe?

Let Jan unpack the suitcase.

Dad will repaint the jeep.

LANGUAGE ARTS

Directions: Add a prefix to each root word. Write the new word on the line.

_____
re + build = _____

_____
un + happy = _____

_____
re + play = _____

_____
un + plug = _____

_____
re + write = _____

_____
un + wrap = _____

LANGUAGE ARTS

A **suffix** is added to the end of a root word. It changes the word's meaning.

The suffix **-ful** means **full of**.

Example: **joyful = full of** joy

The suffix **-ed** means that something happened **in the past**.

Example: We walk**ed** to school.

Directions: Write the root word and the suffix for each **bold** word.

_____

Ana painted her bike.

_____

_____

The book ended sadly.

_____

_____

My tooth is painful when I wiggle it.

_____

_____

I need a cupful of milk.

_____

_____

I picked out a gift.

_____

Directions: Add the suffix **-ful** or **-ed** to each **bold** word below. The meaning of the sentence will help you decide which to add.

The goat **walk**_____ up to us.

Mom **fix**_____ the flat tire quickly.

Can I have a **hand**_____ of peanuts?

The movie **last**_____ for two hours.

Marcia **spott**_____ the moon in the sky.

That puppy is so **play**_____.

88: Rhyming Words

Words that **rhyme** sound alike. The middle and ending sound is the same.

Examples: man pan

Directions: Name the first picture. Circle the word in each row that rhymes with it.

mop   **bag**   **bat**

map   **bed**   **dog**

rock   **top**   **drum**

LANGUAGE ARTS

Directions: Draw a line between the rhyming picture names.

cat

sled

truck

spoon

moon

bat

bed

duck

LANGUAGE ARTS

Directions: Use a **red** crayon to color the things that are usually **red**.

LANGUAGE ARTS

Directions: Draw 3 things that are usually **red**.

LANGUAGE ARTS

Skill 90: Color Words: Orange

Directions: Use an **orange** crayon to color the things that are usually **orange**.

LANGUAGE ARTS

Directions: Draw 3 things that are usually **orange**.

LANGUAGE ARTS

Directions: Use a **yellow** crayon to color the things that are usually **yellow**.

Directions: Draw 3 things that are usually **yellow**.

Directions: Use a **green** crayon to color the things that are usually **green**.

LANGUAGE ARTS

Directions: Draw 3 things that are usually **green**.

LANGUAGE ARTS

Directions: Color the big fish **blue**. Color the small fish **green**.

Directions: Color each space the correct color. Finish coloring the picture.

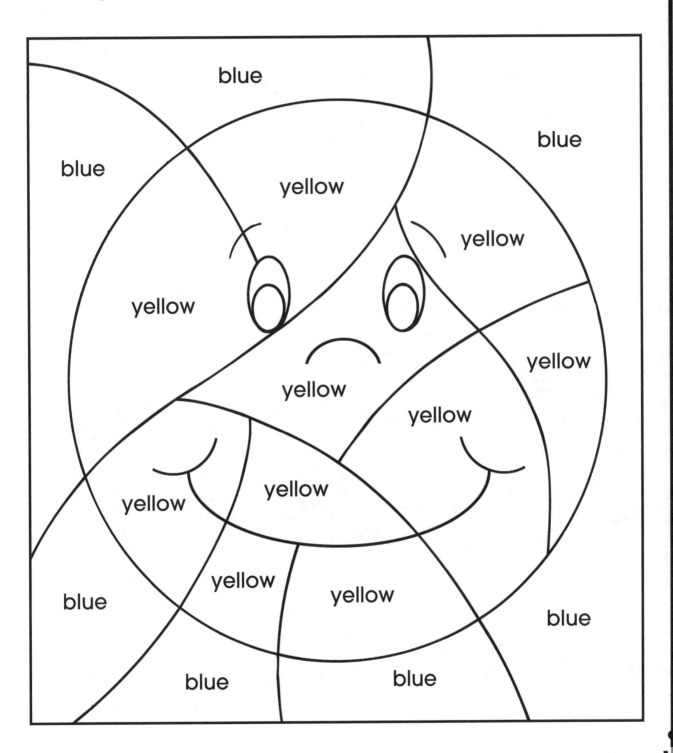

LANGUAGE ARTS

193

Directions: Use a **purple** crayon to color the things that could be **purple**.

Directions: Color each space the correct color. Finish coloring the picture.

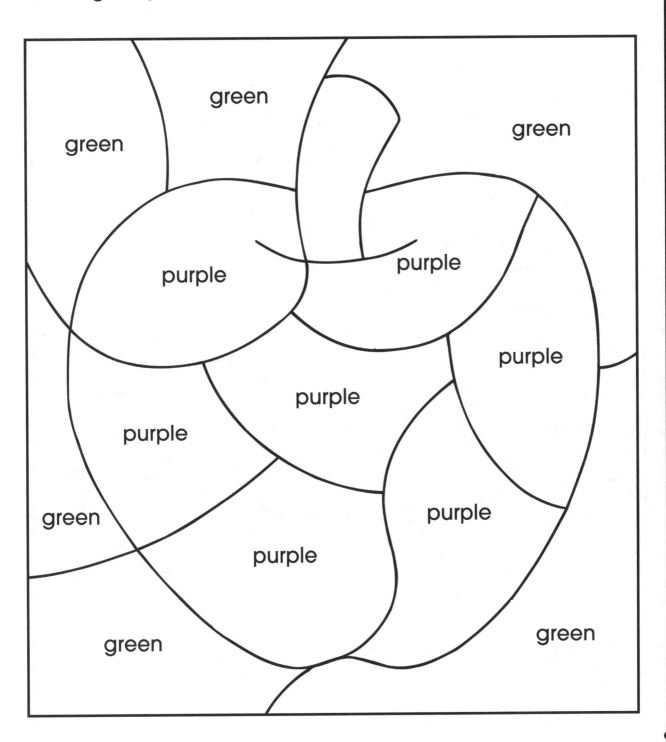

LANGUAGE ARTS

Directions: Color each space the correct color. Finish coloring the picture.

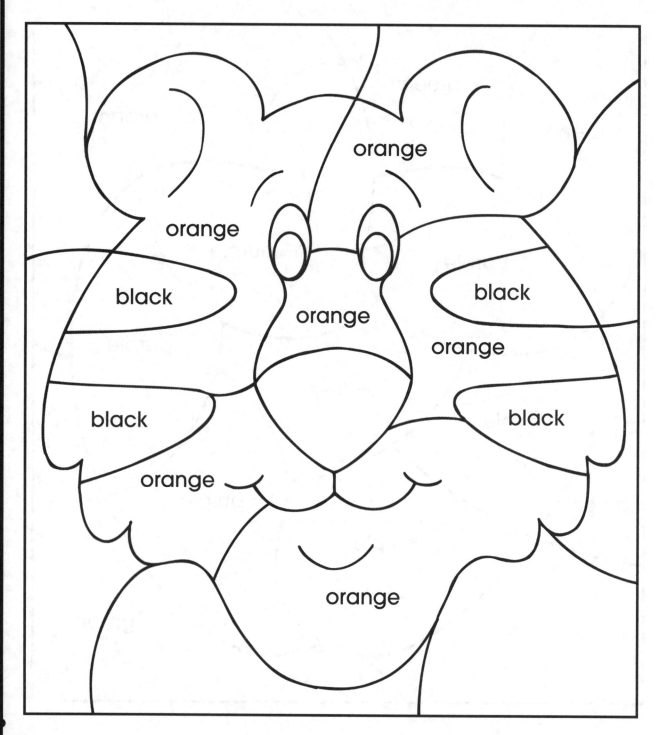

Directions: Color each space the correct color. Finish coloring the picture.

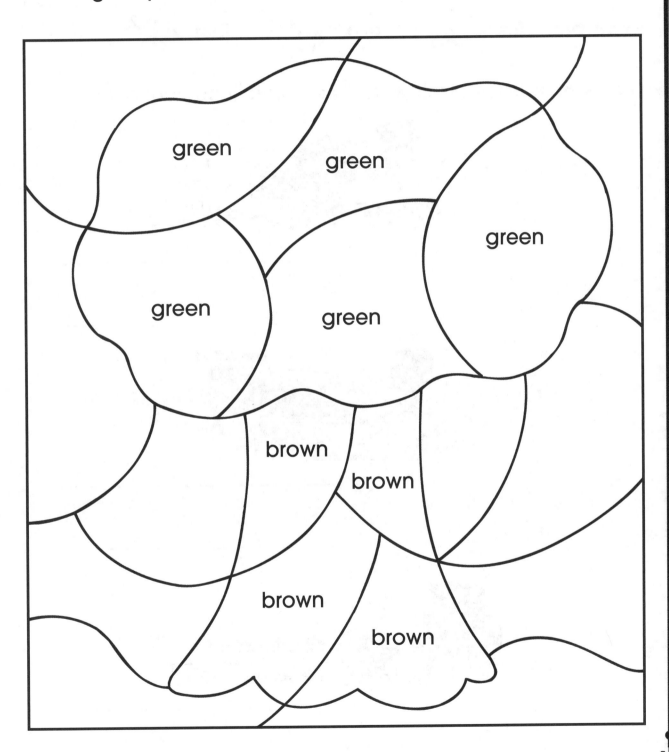

LANGUAGE ARTS

Some words tell in what order things happen. **First**, **next**, and **last** are order words.

Example: **first** **next** **last**

Directions: Trace each word. Then, write it on your own.

first _____

next _____

last _____

Before and **after** are also order words.

Example: **before** **after**

Directions: Look at each before picture. Draw a picture of what might happen after.

Before	**After**

LANGUAGE ARTS

Directions: Circle the words that match the first word.

top	cap	**top**	**top**
sun	sun	top	sun
pig	top	**pig**	**pig**
bed	**bed**	**bed**	pig
cub	cap	**cub**	**cub**

LANGUAGE ARTS

Directions: Circle the words that match the first word.

do	do	you	do
you	the	you	do
sing	you	sing	sing
the	the	you	the
cake	cake	taste	cake

Directions: Trace each number. Then, write it on your own.

1 ___ 2 ___ 3 ___ 4 ___

Directions: Look at each picture. Which happened first? Which happened last? Show the order. Write **1**, **2**, **3**, or **4** under each picture.

_____

_____

_____

_____

Directions: The pictures below are in order. One is missing. What do you think happens in that picture? Draw it.

1

2

3

4

LANGUAGE ARTS

Antonyms are opposites.

Examples:

 **big** **small**   **up** **down**

Directions: Draw a line to match each picture to its antonym.

day

empty

full

winter

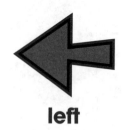

left

night

summer

right

LANGUAGE ARTS

Directions: Look at each antonym pair. Fill in the missing letters. Use the words in the box to help you.

stop	open	tall	in

 closed   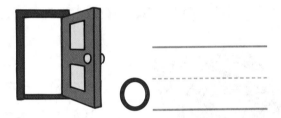 o _____

 go   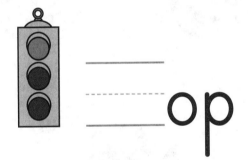 __ __op

 short   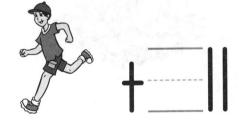 t __ ll

 out   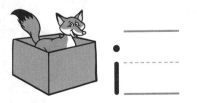 i __

LANGUAGE ARTS

Words that are like each other can be put in a group.

Example: **Foods:** apple , sandwich ,

soup , pizza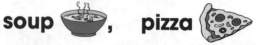

Directions: Make a circle around the animal words. Make a line under things you find in a house.

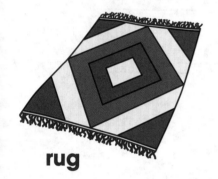

rug

octopus

fish

frog

bed

cat

couch

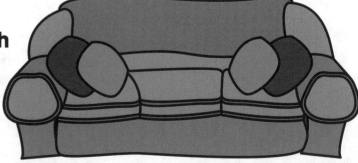

LANGUAGE ARTS

Directions: Draw a line from each word to the group it belongs in.

School Words

Outside Words

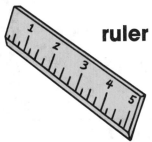

ruler

leaves

pencil

bird

tree

book

LANGUAGE ARTS

Answer Key

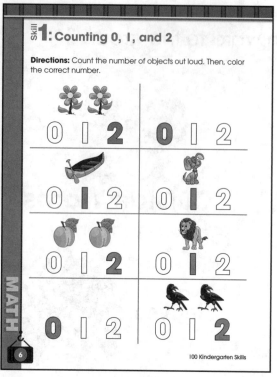

Page 6

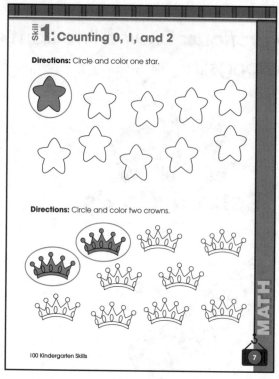

Page 7

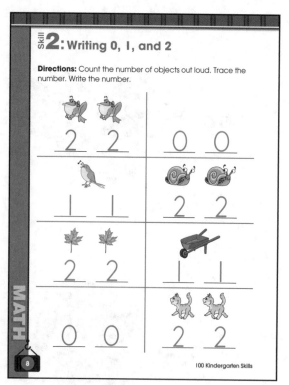

Page 8

Page 9

Answer Key

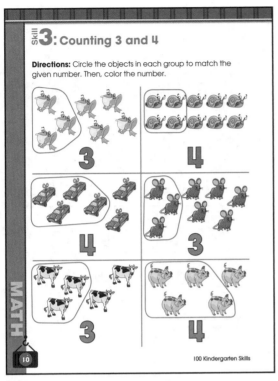

Page 10

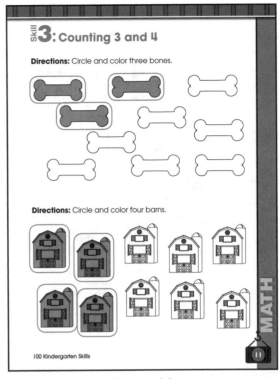

Page 11

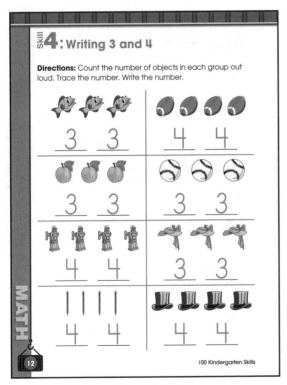

Page 12

Page 13

Answer Key

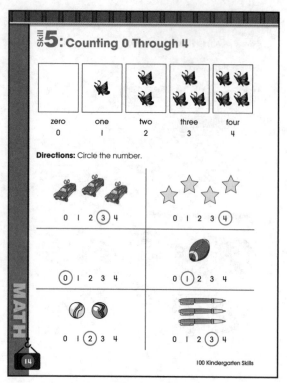

Page 14

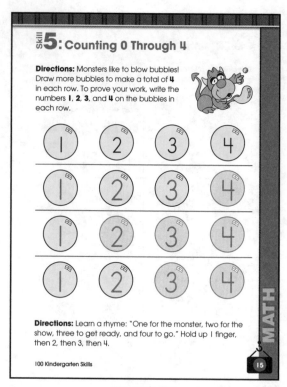

Page 15

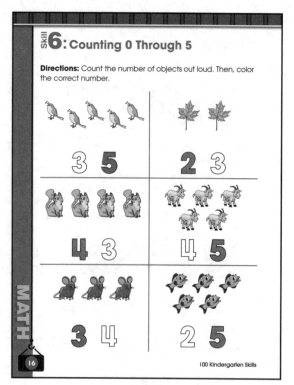

Page 16

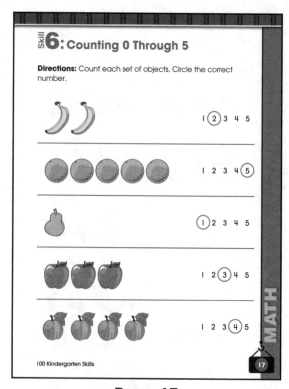

Page 17

Answer Key

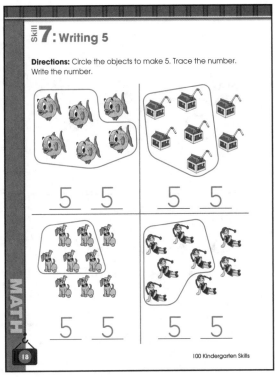

Page 18

Page 19

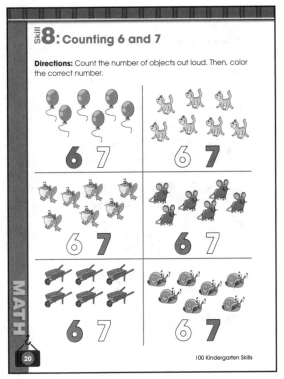

Page 20

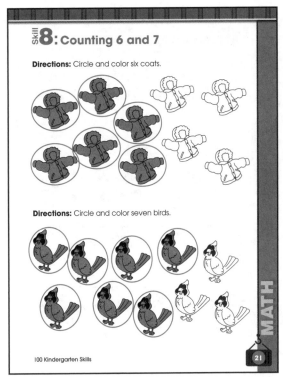

Page 21

Answer Key

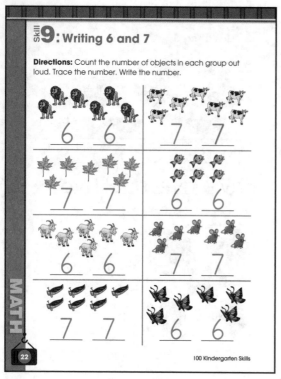

Page 22

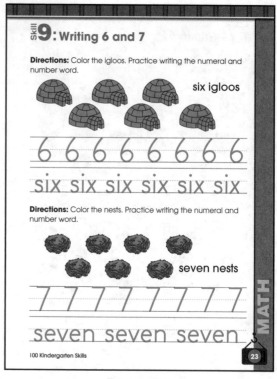

Page 23

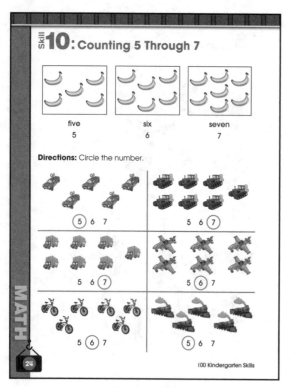

Page 24

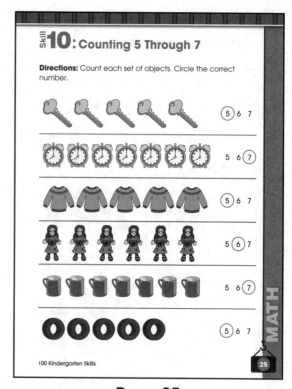

Page 25

Answer Key

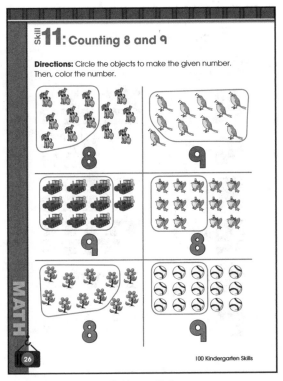

Page 26

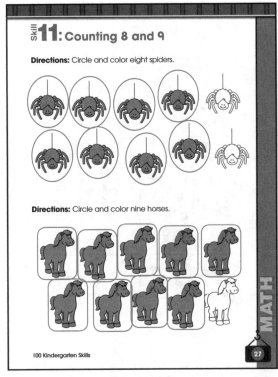

Page 27

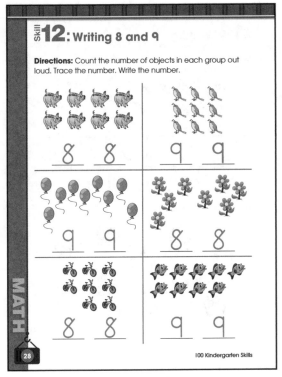

Page 28

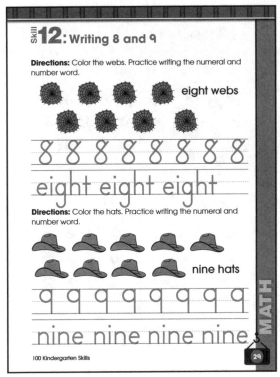

Page 29

Answer Key

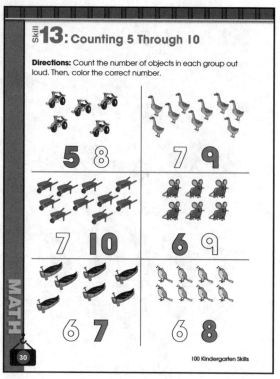

Page 30

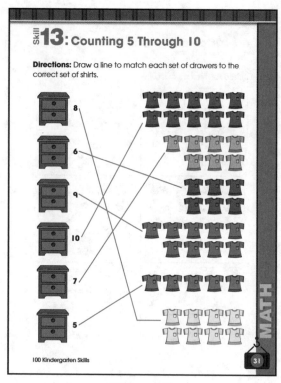

Page 31

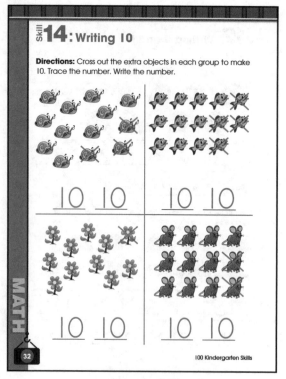

Page 32

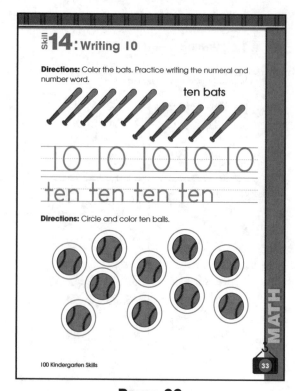

Page 33

Answer Key

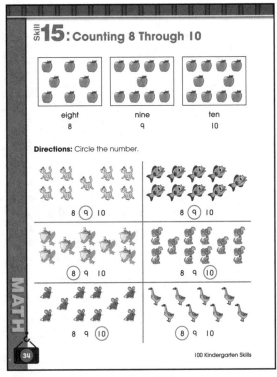

Page 34

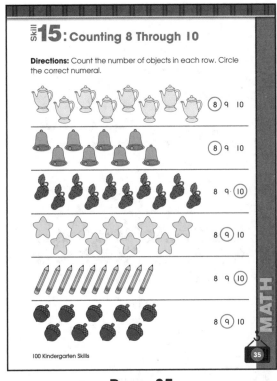

Page 35

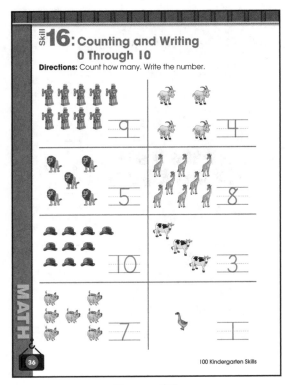

Page 36

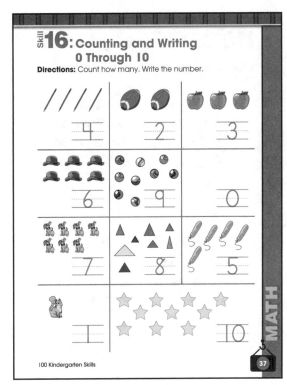

Page 37

Answer Key

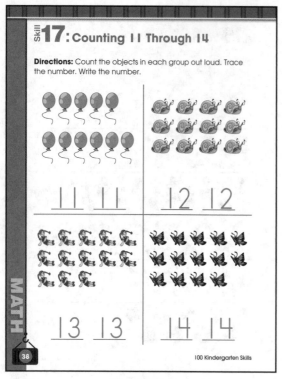

Page 38

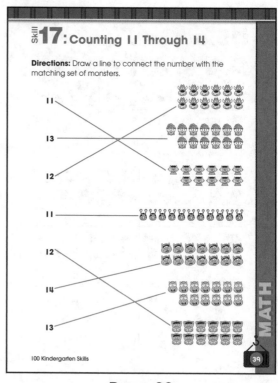

Page 39

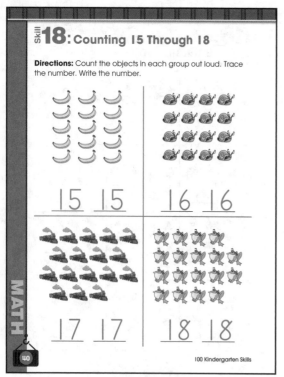

Page 40

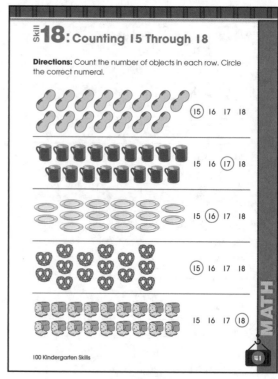

Page 41

Answer Key

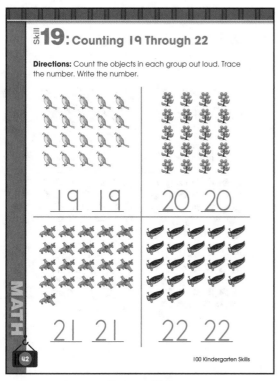

Page 42

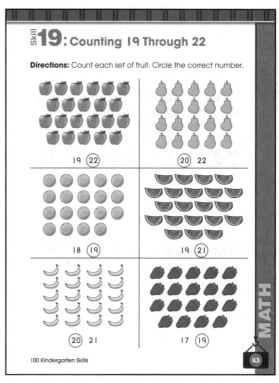

Page 43

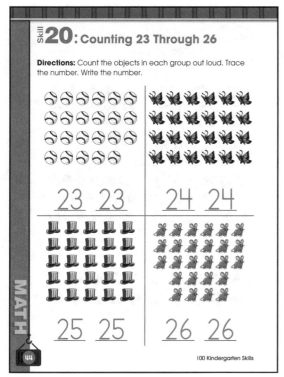

Page 44

Skill 20: Counting 23 Through 26

Directions: Draw the correct number of items in each box.

| 23 apples | 24 flowers |
| 25 frogs | 26 balloons |

Page 45

Answer Key

Skill 21: Counting 27 Through 30

Directions: Count the objects in each group out loud. Trace the number. Write the number.

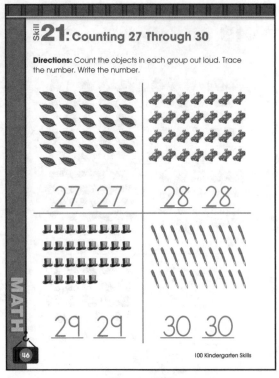

Page 46

Skill 21: Counting 27 Through 30

Directions: Count each set. Write the correct number in each box.

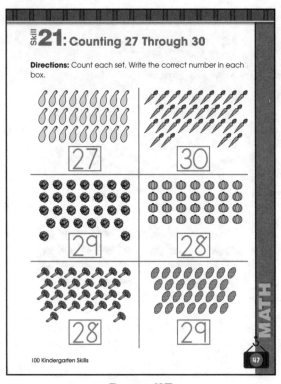

Page 47

Skill 22: Counting and Writing 11 Through 20

Directions: Count how many. Trace the number.

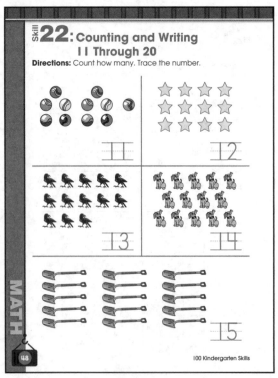

Page 48

Skill 22: Counting and Writing 11 Through 20

Directions: Count how many. Trace the number.

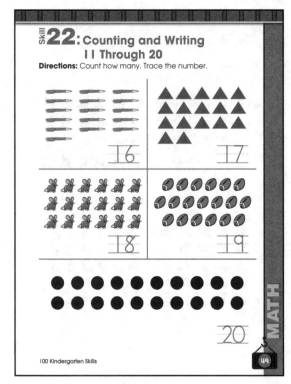

Page 49

Answer Key

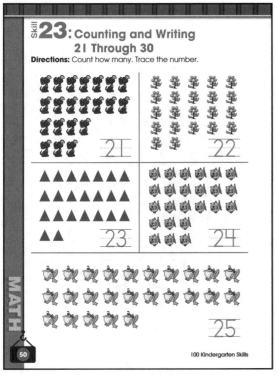

Page 50

Page 51

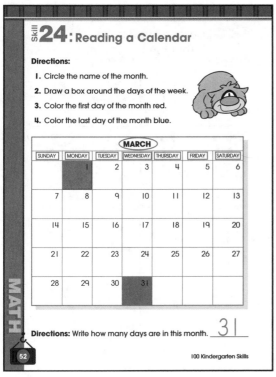

Page 52

Page 53

Answer Key

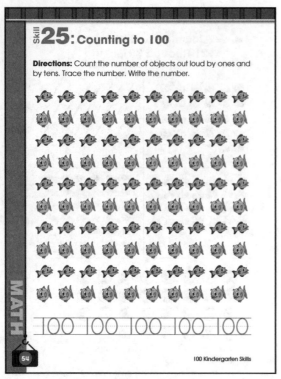

Page 54

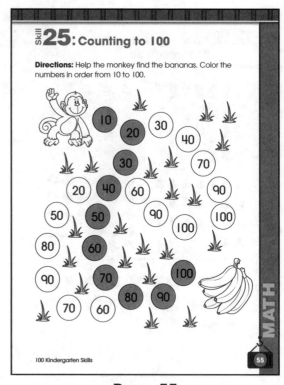

Page 55

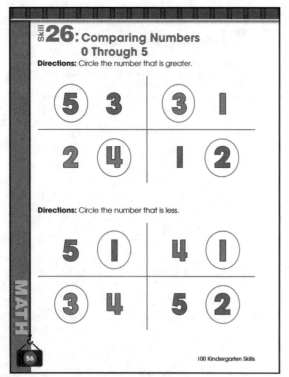

Page 56

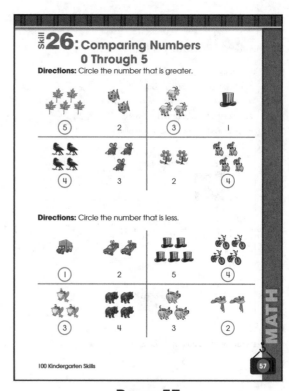

Page 57

Answer Key

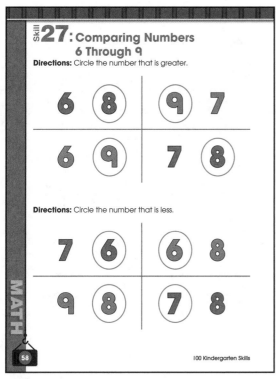

Skill 27: Comparing Numbers 6 Through 9

Directions: Circle the number that is greater.

Directions: Circle the number that is less.

Page 58

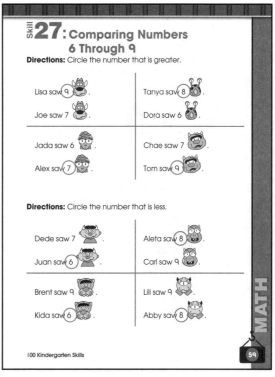

Skill 27: Comparing Numbers 6 Through 9

Directions: Circle the number that is greater.

Lisa saw ⑨ .   Tanya saw ⑧ .
Joe saw 7 .   Dora saw 6 .

Jada saw 6 .   Chae saw 7 .
Alex saw ⑦ .   Tom saw ⑨ .

Directions: Circle the number that is less.

Dede saw 7 .   Aleta saw ⑧ .
Juan saw ⑥ .   Carl saw 9 .

Brent saw 9 .   Lili saw 9 .
Kida saw ⑥ .   Abby saw ⑧ .

Page 59

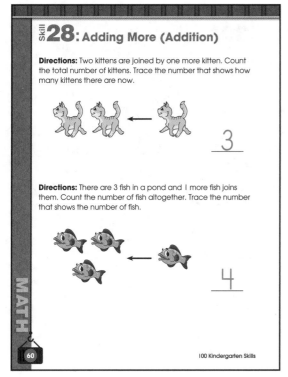

Skill 28: Adding More (Addition)

Directions: Two kittens are joined by one more kitten. Count the total number of kittens. Trace the number that shows how many kittens there are now.

3

Directions: There are 3 fish in a pond and 1 more fish joins them. Count the number of fish altogether. Trace the number that shows the number of fish.

4

Page 60

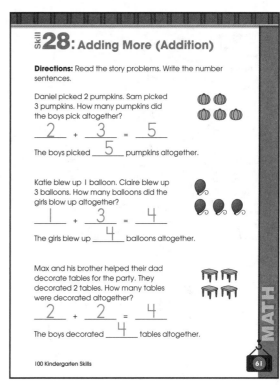

Skill 28: Adding More (Addition)

Directions: Read the story problems. Write the number sentences.

Daniel picked 2 pumpkins. Sam picked 3 pumpkins. How many pumpkins did the boys pick altogether?

$\underline{2} + \underline{3} = \underline{5}$

The boys picked __5__ pumpkins altogether.

Katie blew up 1 balloon. Claire blew up 3 balloons. How many balloons did the girls blow up altogether?

$\underline{1} + \underline{3} = \underline{4}$

The girls blew up __4__ balloons altogether.

Max and his brother helped their dad decorate tables for the party. They decorated 2 tables. How many tables were decorated altogether?

$\underline{2} + \underline{2} = \underline{4}$

The boys decorated __4__ tables altogether.

Page 61

Answer Key

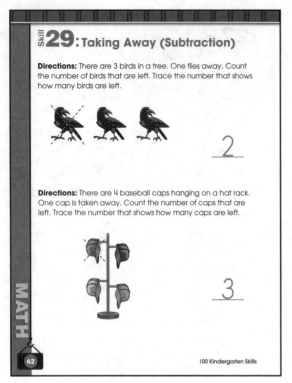

Skill 29: Taking Away (Subtraction)

Directions: There are 3 birds in a tree. One flies away. Count the number of birds that are left. Trace the number that shows how many birds are left.

2

Directions: There are 4 baseball caps hanging on a hat rack. One cap is taken away. Count the number of caps that are left. Trace the number that shows how many caps are left.

3

100 Kindergarten Skills

62

Page 62

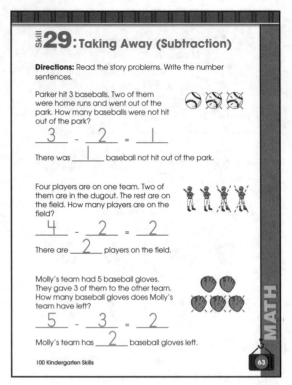

Skill 29: Taking Away (Subtraction)

Directions: Read the story problems. Write the number sentences.

Parker hit 3 baseballs. Two of them were home runs and went out of the park. How many baseballs were not hit out of the park?

3 - 2 = 1

There was ___1___ baseball not hit out of the park.

Four players are on one team. Two of them are in the dugout. The rest are on the field. How many players are on the field?

4 - 2 = 2

There are ___2___ players on the field.

Molly's team had 5 baseball gloves. They gave 3 of them to the other team. How many baseball gloves does Molly's team have left?

5 - 3 = 2

Molly's team has ___2___ baseball gloves left.

100 Kindergarten Skills

63

Page 63

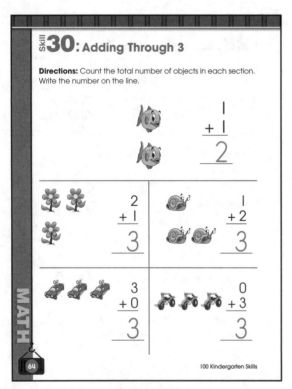

Skill 30: Adding Through 3

Directions: Count the total number of objects in each section. Write the number on the line.

+ 1
———
2

2
+ 1
———
3

1
+ 2
———
3

3
+ 0
———
3

0
+ 3
———
3

100 Kindergarten Skills

64

Page 64

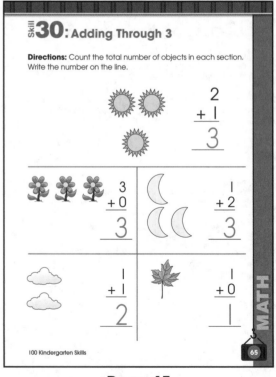

Skill 30: Adding Through 3

Directions: Count the total number of objects in each section. Write the number on the line.

2
+ 1
———
3

3
+ 0
———
3

1
+ 2
———
3

1
+ 1
———
2

1
+ 0
———
1

100 Kindergarten Skills

65

Page 65

Answer Key

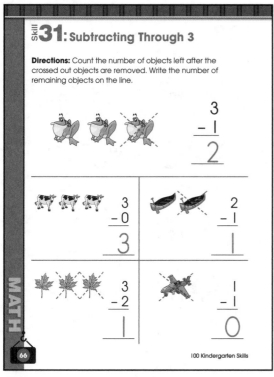

Page 66

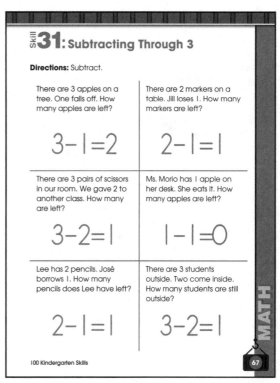

Page 67

Page 68

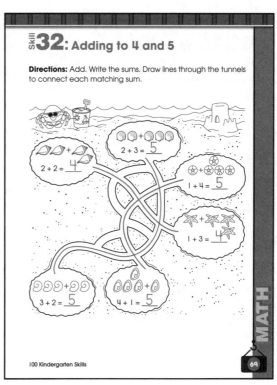

Page 69

Answer Key

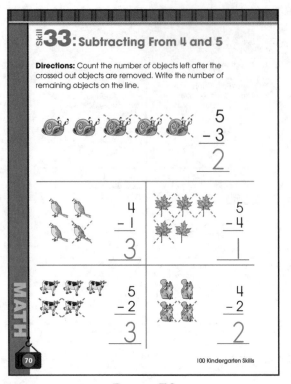

Page 70

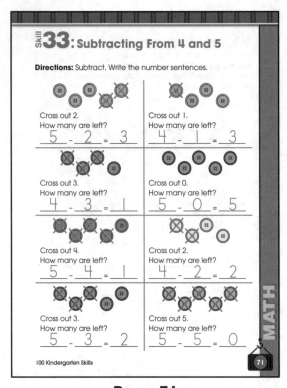

Page 71

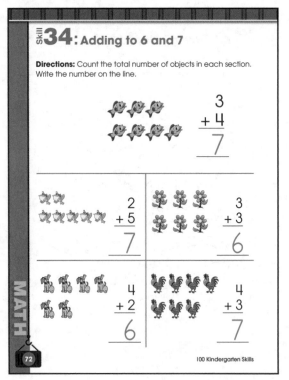

Page 72

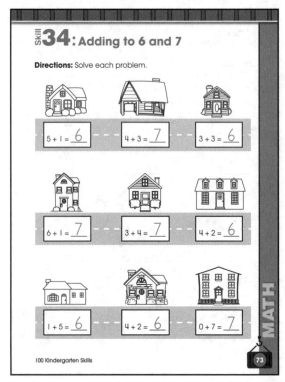

Page 73

Answer Key

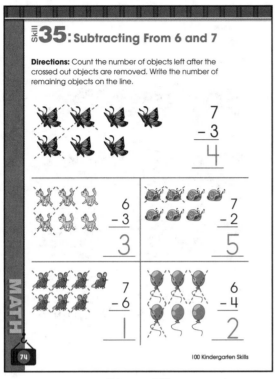

Page 74

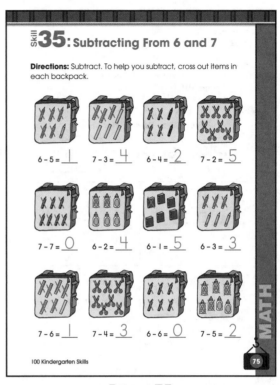

Page 75

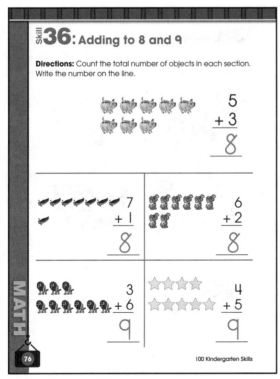

Page 76

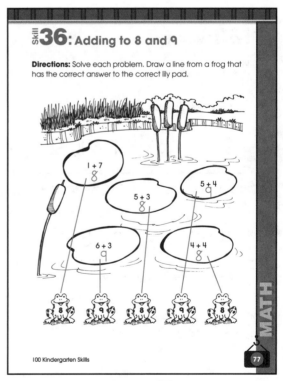

Page 77

Answer Key

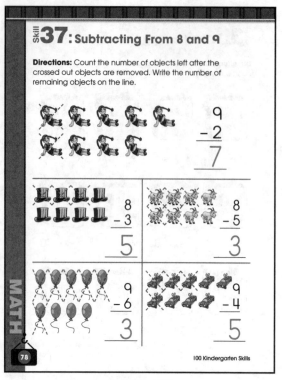

Skill 37: Subtracting From 8 and 9

Directions: Count the number of objects left after the crossed out objects are removed. Write the number of remaining objects on the line.

$$-2 \over 7$$ 9

$$8 - 3 \over 5$$

$$8 - 5 \over 3$$

$$9 - 6 \over 3$$

$$9 - 4 \over 5$$

100 Kindergarten Skills
78

Page 78

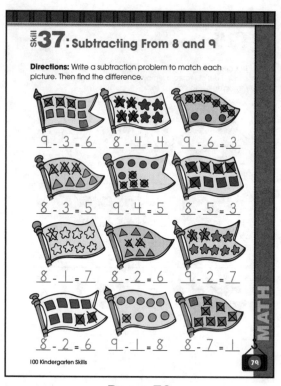

Skill 37: Subtracting From 8 and 9

Directions: Write a subtraction problem to match each picture. Then find the difference.

$9 - 3 = 6$ $8 - 4 = 4$ $9 - 6 = 3$

$8 - 3 = 5$ $9 - 4 = 5$ $8 - 5 = 3$

$8 - 1 = 7$ $8 - 2 = 6$ $9 - 2 = 7$

$8 - 2 = 6$ $9 - 1 = 8$ $8 - 7 = 1$

100 Kindergarten Skills
79

Page 79

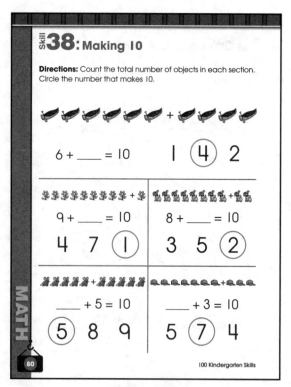

Skill 38: Making 10

Directions: Count the total number of objects in each section. Circle the number that makes 10.

$6 + \underline{} = 10$ 1 ④ 2

$9 + \underline{} = 10$ 4 7 ①
$8 + \underline{} = 10$ 3 5 ②

$\underline{} + 5 = 10$ ⑤ 8 9
$\underline{} + 3 = 10$ 5 ⑦ 4

100 Kindergarten Skills
80

Page 80

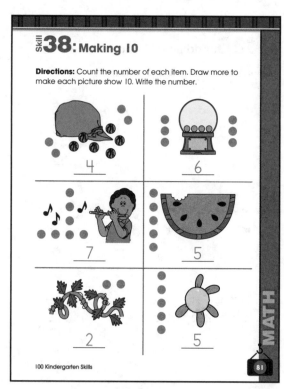

Skill 38: Making 10

Directions: Count the number of each item. Draw more to make each picture show 10. Write the number.

4   6

7   5

2   5

100 Kindergarten Skills
81

Page 81

Answer Key

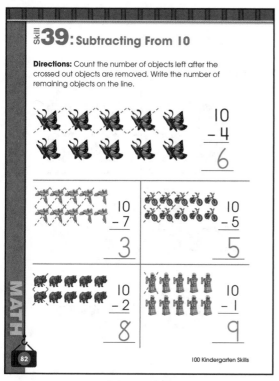

Page 82

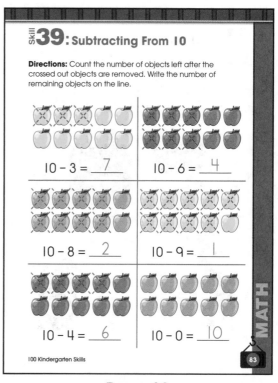

Page 83

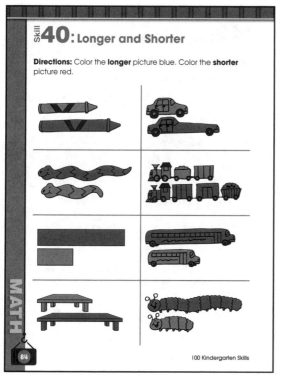

Page 84

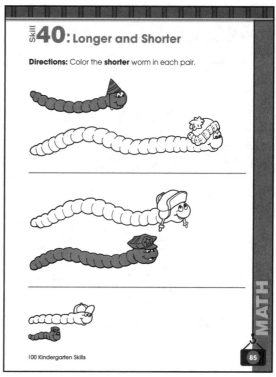

Page 85

Answer Key

Page 86

Page 87

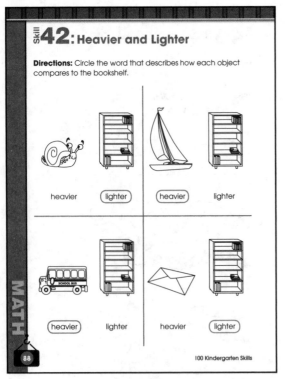

Page 88

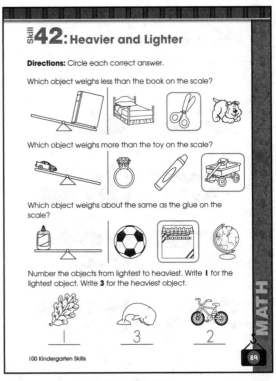

Page 89

Answer Key

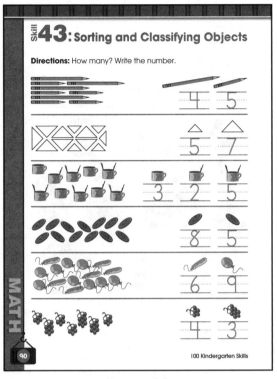

Skill 43: Sorting and Classifying Objects

Directions: How many? Write the number.

Page 90

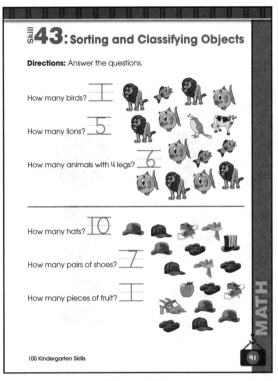

Skill 43: Sorting and Classifying Objects

Directions: Answer the questions.

How many birds? I
How many lions? 5
How many animals with 4 legs? 6

How many hats? 10
How many pairs of shoes? 7
How many pieces of fruit? 1

Page 91

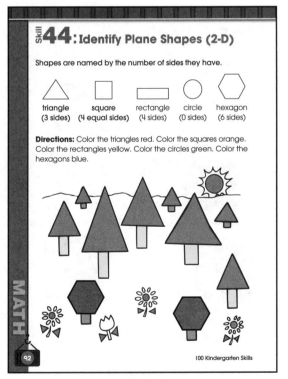

Skill 44: Identify Plane Shapes (2-D)

Shapes are named by the number of sides they have.

triangle (3 sides)   square (4 equal sides)   rectangle (4 sides)   circle (0 sides)   hexagon (6 sides)

Directions: Color the triangles red. Color the squares orange. Color the rectangles yellow. Color the circles green. Color the hexagons blue.

Page 92

Skill 44: Identify Plane Shapes (2-D)

Directions: Color the squares green. Color the rectangles yellow. Color the circles red. Color the triangles blue.

Page 93

Answer Key

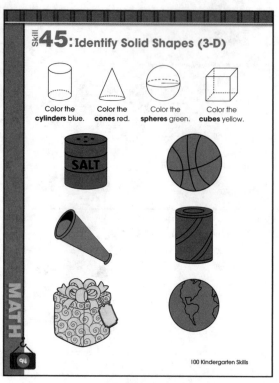

Page 94

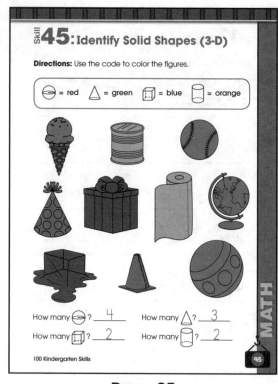

Page 95

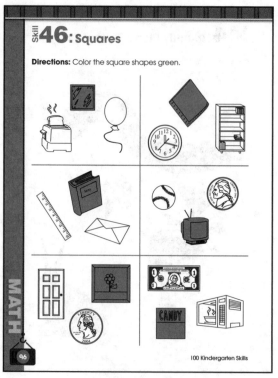

Page 96

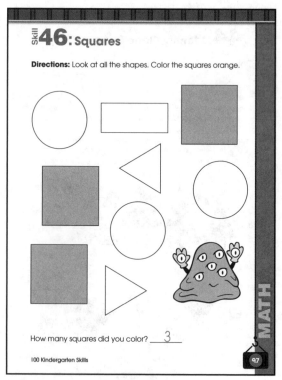

Page 97

Answer Key

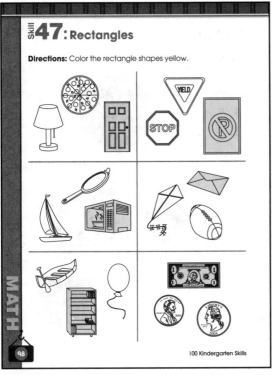

Page 98

Page 99

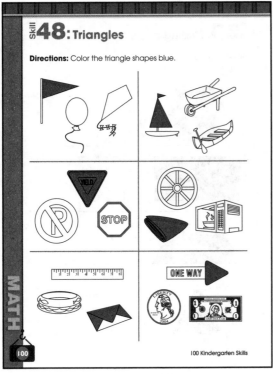

Page 100

Page 101

Answer Key

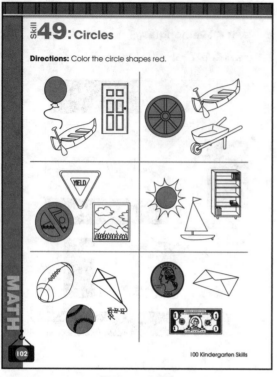

Skill 49: Circles

Directions: Color the circle shapes red.

100 Kindergarten Skills

102

Page 102

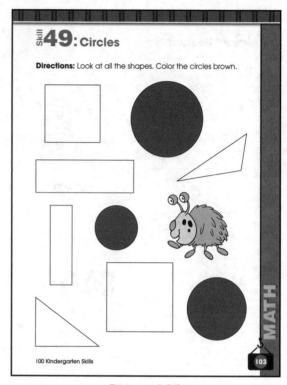

Skill 49: Circles

Directions: Look at all the shapes. Color the circles brown.

100 Kindergarten Skills

103

Page 103

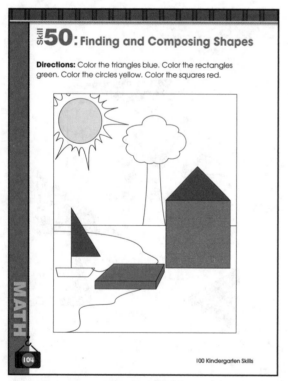

Skill 50: Finding and Composing Shapes

Directions: Color the triangles blue. Color the rectangles green. Color the circles yellow. Color the squares red.

100 Kindergarten Skills

104

Page 104

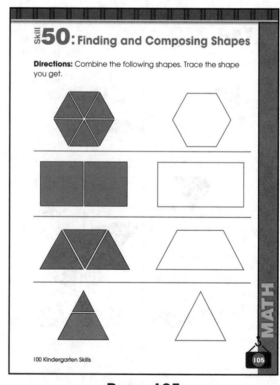

Skill 50: Finding and Composing Shapes

Directions: Combine the following shapes. Trace the shape you get.

100 Kindergarten Skills

105

Page 105

Answer Key

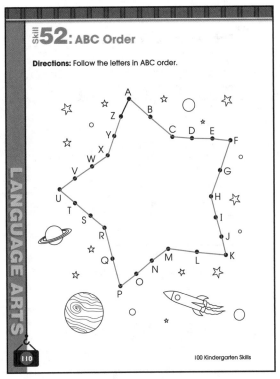

Page 110

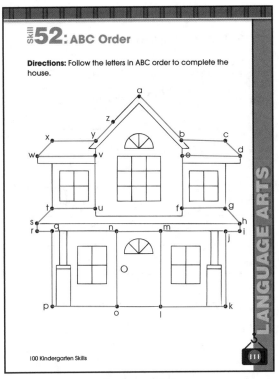

Page 111

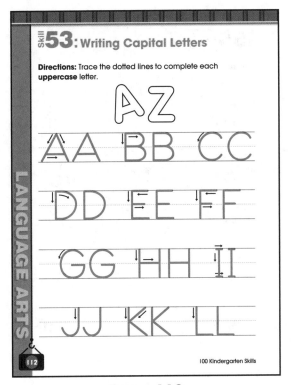

Page 112

Page 113

Answer Key

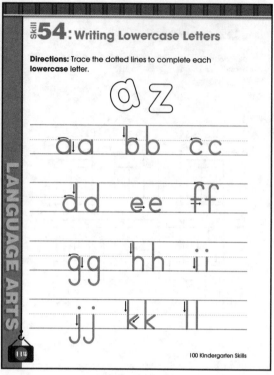

Page 114

Page 115

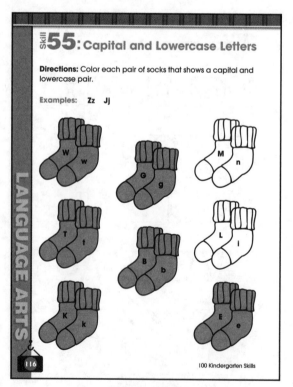

Page 116

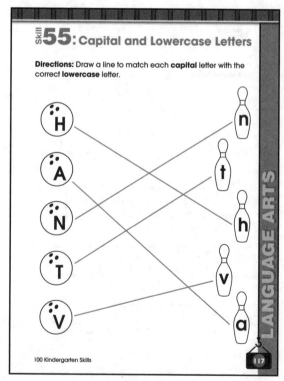

Page 117

Answer Key

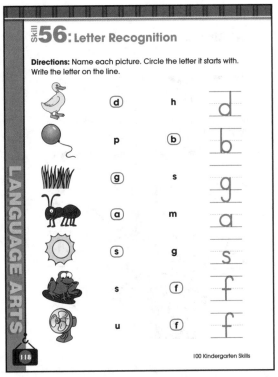

Page 118

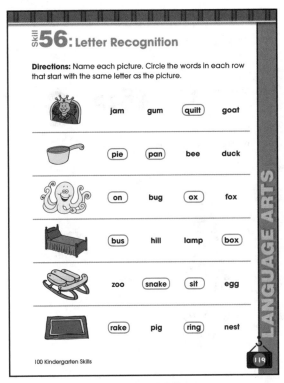

Page 119

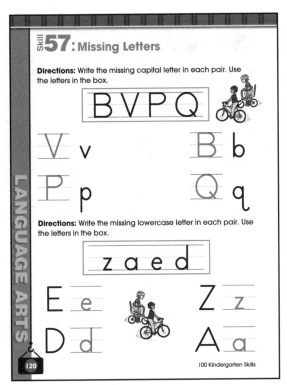

Page 120

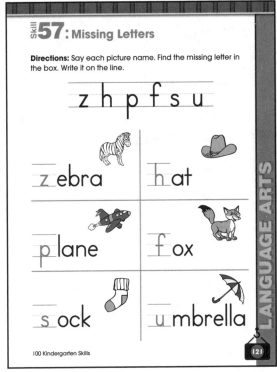

Page 121

Answer Key

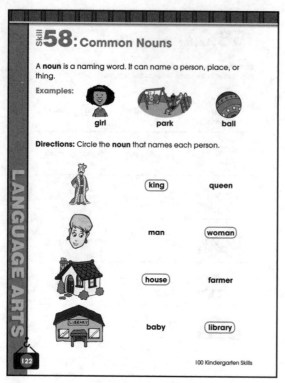

Page 122

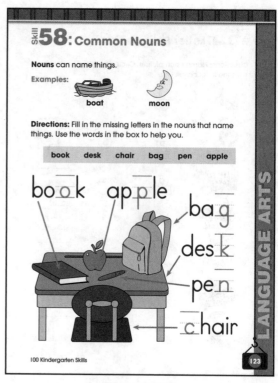

Page 123

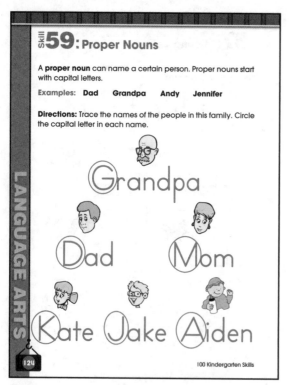

Page 124

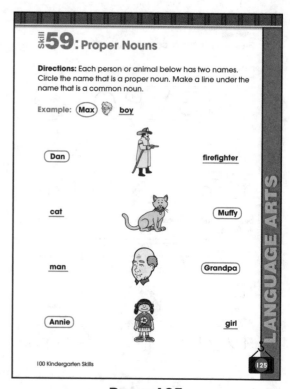

Page 125

Answer Key

Skill 60: Verbs

A **verb** is an action word. It tells what happens in a sentence.

Examples: jump   laugh   throw

Directions: Anita and Tom are cooking. Circle the action word in each sentence that tells what they do.

Tom (cuts.)

Anita (washes.)

Anita (mixes.)

Anita (stirs.)

Tom (peels.)

They (cook.)

100 Kindergarten Skills

126

Page 126

Skill 60: Verbs

Directions: Name the action words below. Write the missing letters on the lines. Use the words in the box to help you.

| swim | dig | kick | eat | clap |

eat

clap

dig

kick

swim

100 Kindergarten Skills

127

Page 127

Skill 61: Prepositions

A **preposition** can show location (where) or time (when). Prepositions link nouns to other words in a sentence.

Examples: **on** the roof   **in** the cup

Directions: Trace the prepositions that match each picture.

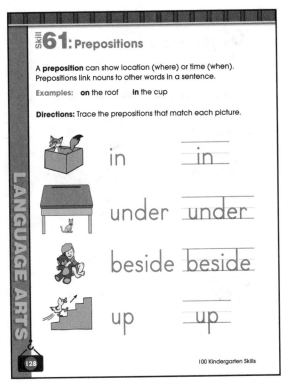

in   in

under   under

beside   beside

up   up

100 Kindergarten Skills

128

Page 128

Skill 61: Prepositions

Directions: Choose a preposition to complete each sentence. Write it on the line.

to, on, with

Sam ran ___to___ the park.

off, into, under

Rex hid __under__ the bed.

at, on, up

Sid's ball is ___on___ the roof.

at, on, under

Mom will be home ___at___ 6:00.

100 Kindergarten Skills

129

Page 129

Answer Key

Page 130

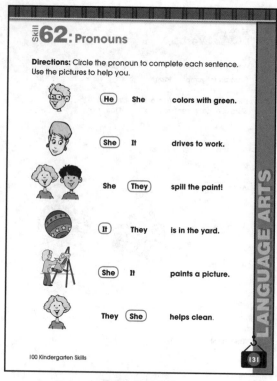

Page 131

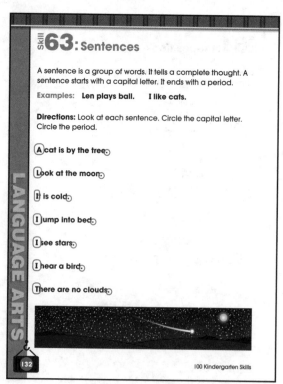

Page 132

Page 133

Answer Key

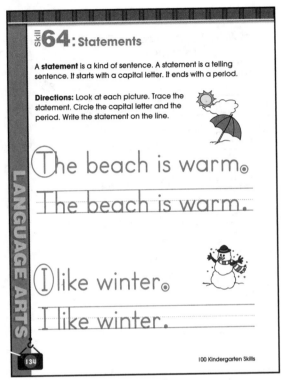

Page 134

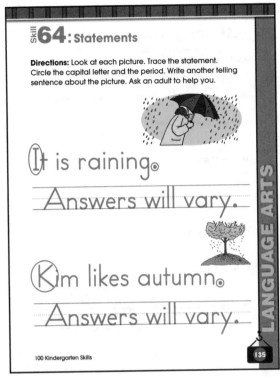

Page 135

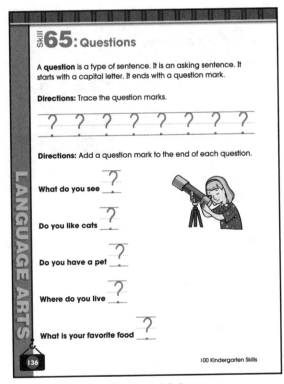

Page 136

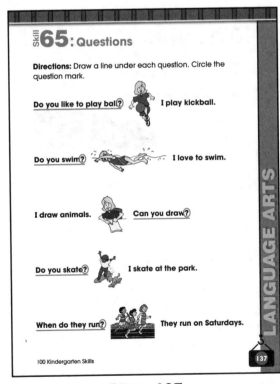

Page 137

Answer Key

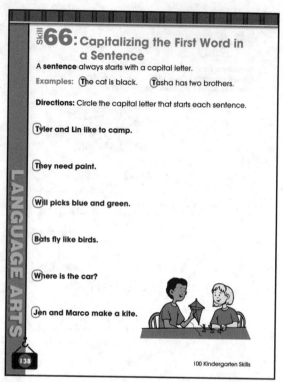

Skill 66: Capitalizing the First Word in a Sentence

A **sentence** always starts with a capital letter.

Examples: (T)he cat is black. (T)asha has two brothers.

Directions: Circle the capital letter that starts each sentence.

(T)yler and Lin like to camp.

(T)hey need paint.

(W)ill picks blue and green.

(B)ats fly like birds.

(W)here is the car?

(J)en and Marco make a kite.

138

100 Kindergarten Skills

Page 138

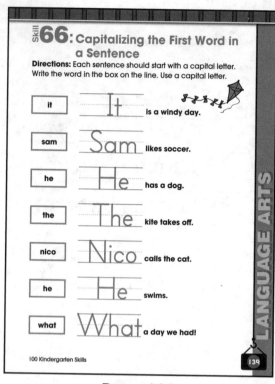

Skill 66: Capitalizing the First Word in a Sentence

Directions: Each sentence should start with a capital letter. Write the word in the box on the line. Use a capital letter.

it	It	is a windy day.
sam	Sam	likes soccer.
he	He	has a dog.
the	The	kite takes off.
nico	Nico	calls the cat.
he	He	swims.
what	What	a day we had!

100 Kindergarten Skills

139

Page 139

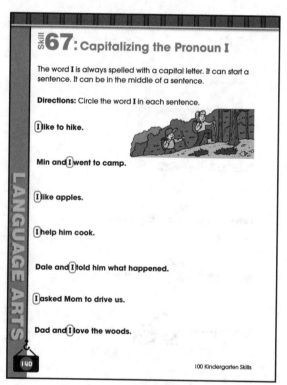

Skill 67: Capitalizing the Pronoun I

The word **I** is always spelled with a capital letter. It can start a sentence. It can be in the middle of a sentence.

Directions: Circle the word **I** in each sentence.

(I) like to hike.

Min and (I) went to camp.

(I) like apples.

(I) help him cook.

Dale and (I) told him what happened.

(I) asked Mom to drive us.

Dad and (I) love the woods.

140

100 Kindergarten Skills

Page 140

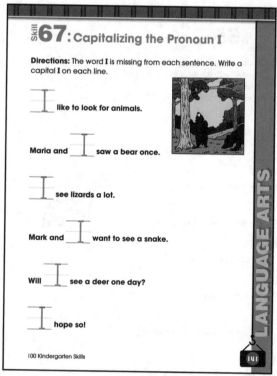

Skill 67: Capitalizing the Pronoun I

Directions: The word **I** is missing from each sentence. Write a capital **I** on each line.

I like to look for animals.

Maria and I saw a bear once.

I see lizards a lot.

Mark and I want to see a snake.

Will I see a deer one day?

I hope so!

100 Kindergarten Skills

141

Page 141

Answer Key

Page 142

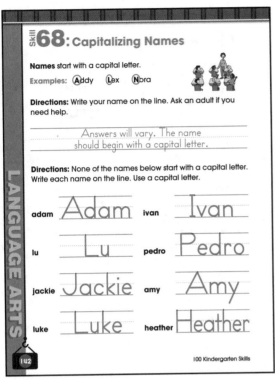

Skill 68: Capitalizing Names

Names start with a capital letter.

Examples: (A)ddy (L)ex (N)ora

Directions: Write your name on the line. Ask an adult if you need help.

Answers will vary. The name should begin with a capital letter.

Directions: None of the names below start with a capital letter. Write each name on the line. Use a capital letter.

adam **Adam**   ivan **Ivan**

lu **Lu**   pedro **Pedro**

jackie **Jackie**   amy **Amy**

luke **Luke**   heather **Heather**

100 Kindergarten Skills

142

Page 143

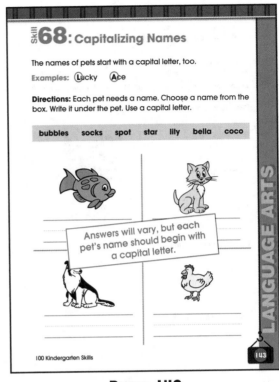

Skill 68: Capitalizing Names

The names of pets start with a capital letter, too.

Examples: (L)ucky (A)ce

Directions: Each pet needs a name. Choose a name from the box. Write it under the pet. Use a capital letter.

| bubbles | socks | spot | star | lily | bella | coco |

Answers will vary, but each pet's name should begin with a capital letter.

100 Kindergarten Skills

143

Page 144

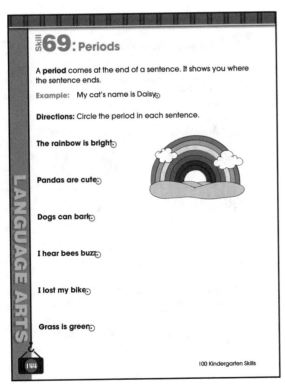

Skill 69: Periods

A **period** comes at the end of a sentence. It shows you where the sentence ends.

Example: My cat's name is Daisy(.)

Directions: Circle the period in each sentence.

The rainbow is bright(.)

Pandas are cute(.)

Dogs can bark(.)

I hear bees buzz(.)

I lost my bike(.)

Grass is green(.)

100 Kindergarten Skills

144

Page 145

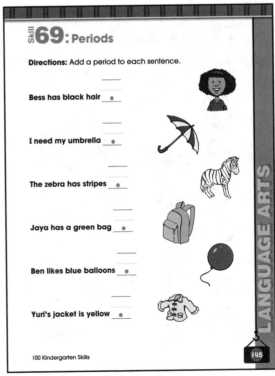

Skill 69: Periods

Directions: Add a period to each sentence.

Bess has black hair ·

I need my umbrella ·

The zebra has stripes ·

Jaya has a green bag ·

Ben likes blue balloons ·

Yuri's jacket is yellow ·

100 Kindergarten Skills

145

Answer Key

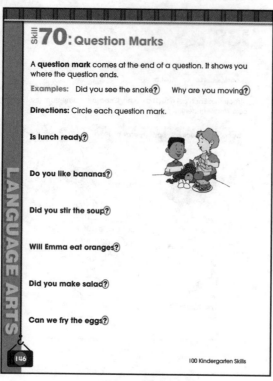

Page 146

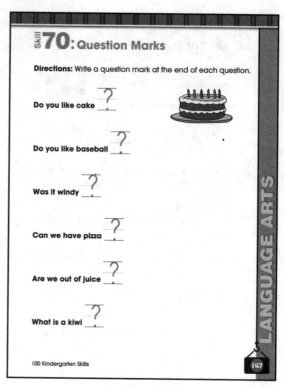

Page 147

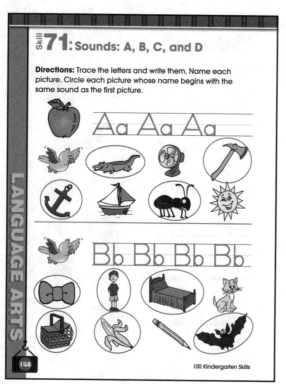

Page 148

Page 149

Answer Key

Page 150

Page 151

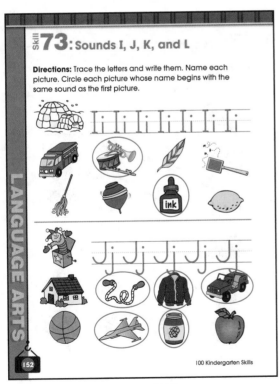

Page 152

Page 153

Answer Key

Page 154

Page 155

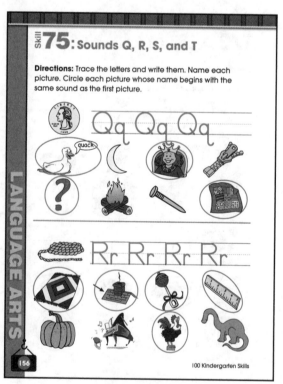

Page 156

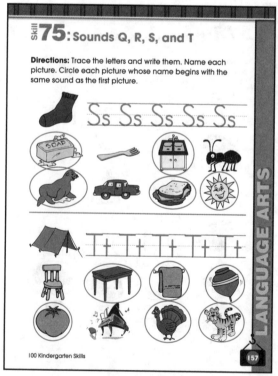

Page 157

Answer Key

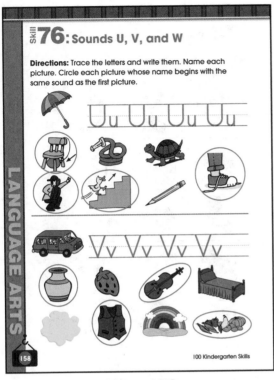

Page 158

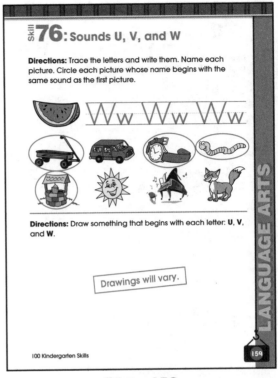

Page 159

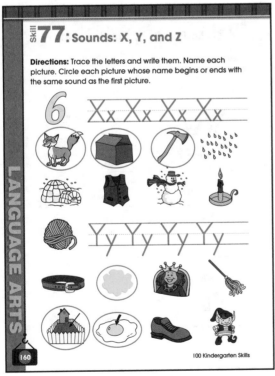

Page 160

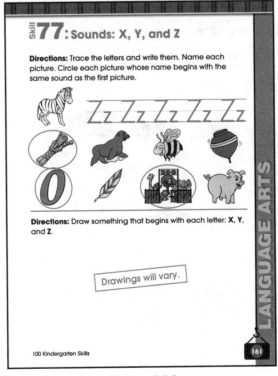

Page 161

Answer Key

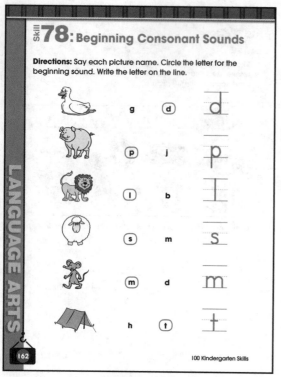

Page 162

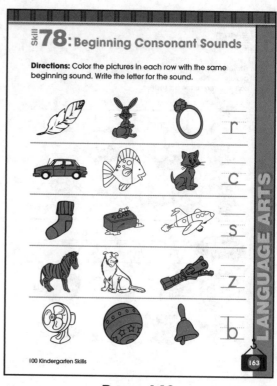

Page 163

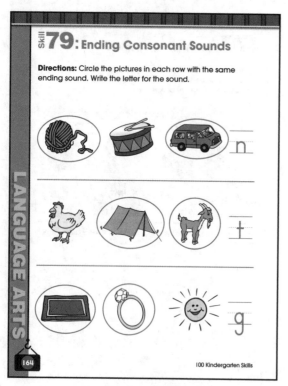

Page 164

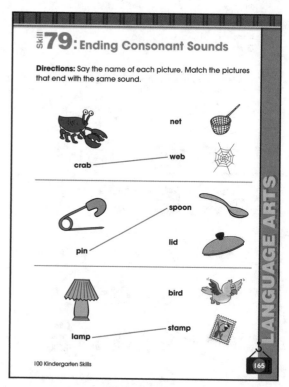

Page 165

Answer Key

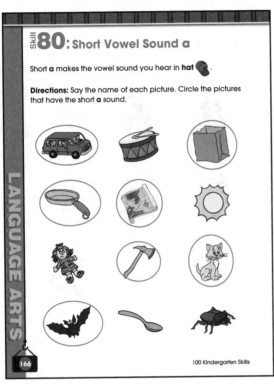

Page 166

Page 167

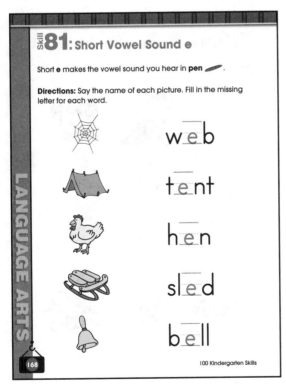

Page 168

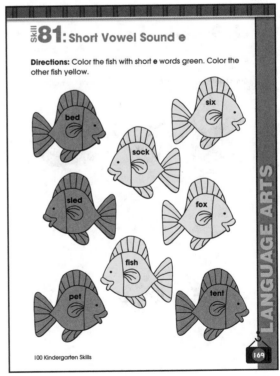

Page 169

Answer Key

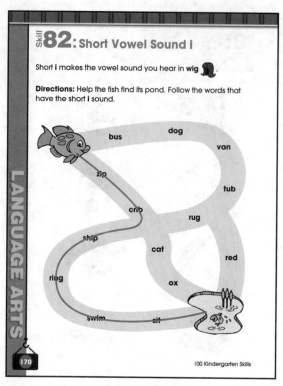

Page 170

Page 171

Page 172

Page 173

Answer Key

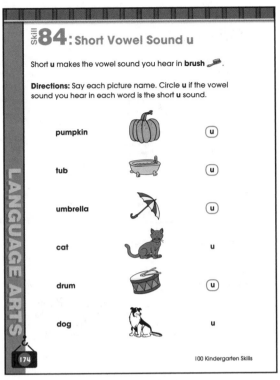

Page 174

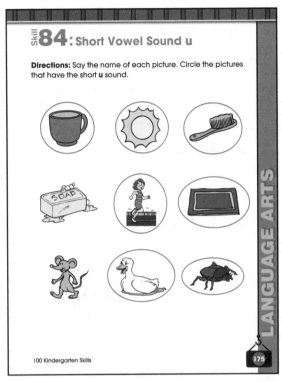

Page 175

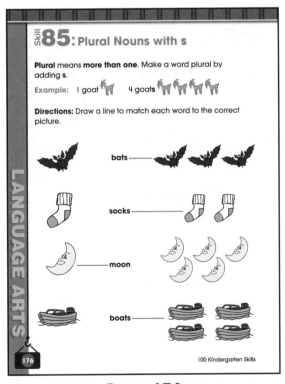

Page 176

Page 177

Answer Key

Page 178

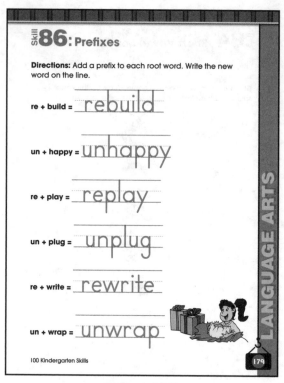

Page 179

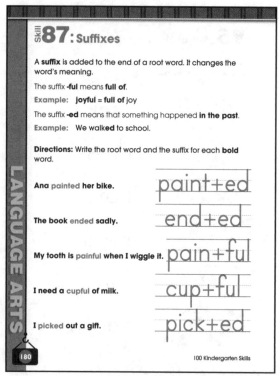

Page 180

Page 181

Answer Key

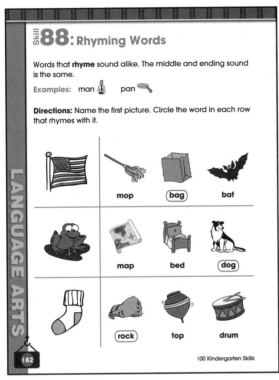

Page 182

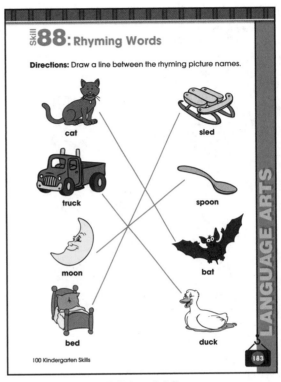

Page 183

Page 184

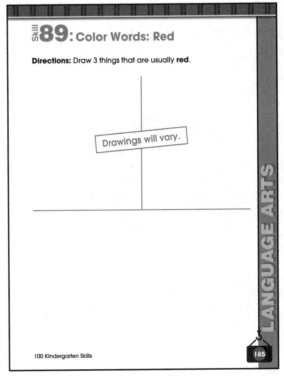

Page 185

Answer Key

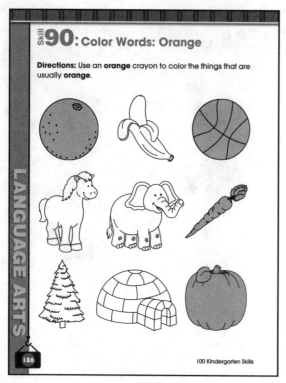

Page 186

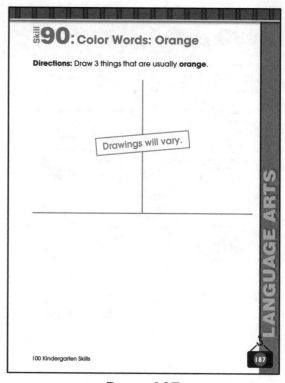

Page 187

Page 188

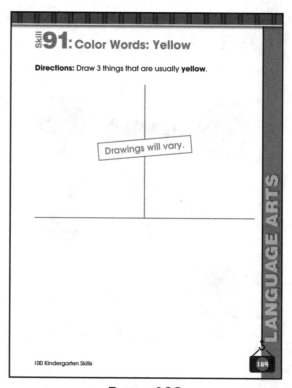

Page 189

Answer Key

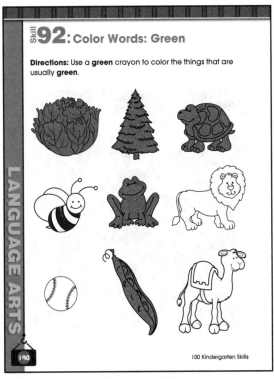

Skill 92: Color Words: Green

Directions: Use a **green** crayon to color the things that are usually **green**.

100 Kindergarten Skills

Page 190

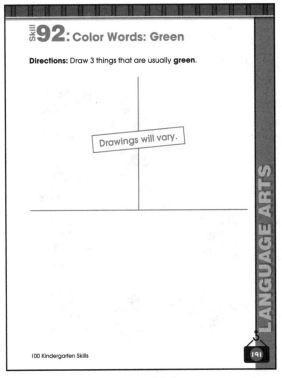

Skill 92: Color Words: Green

Directions: Draw 3 things that are usually **green**.

Drawings will vary.

100 Kindergarten Skills

Page 191

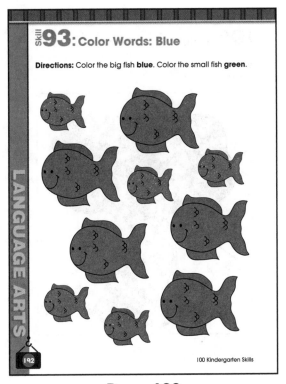

Skill 93: Color Words: Blue

Directions: Color the big fish **blue**. Color the small fish **green**.

100 Kindergarten Skills

Page 192

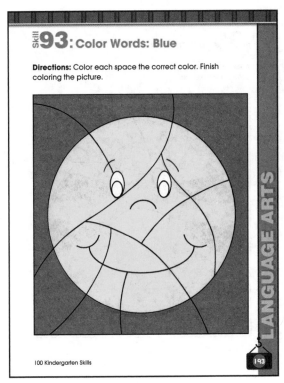

Skill 93: Color Words: Blue

Directions: Color each space the correct color. Finish coloring the picture.

100 Kindergarten Skills

Page 193

Answer Key

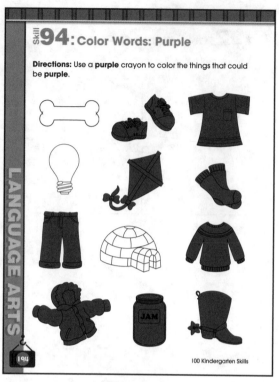

Skill 94: Color Words: Purple

Directions: Use a **purple** crayon to color the things that could be **purple**.

JAM

194

100 Kindergarten Skills

Page 194

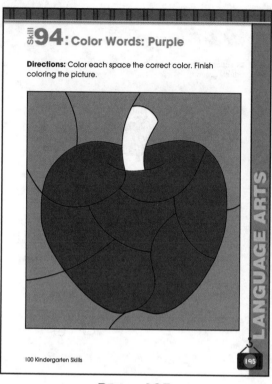

Skill 94: Color Words: Purple

Directions: Color each space the correct color. Finish coloring the picture.

100 Kindergarten Skills

195

Page 195

Skill 95: Color Words: Black and Brown

Directions: Color each space the correct color. Finish coloring the picture.

196

100 Kindergarten Skills

Page 196

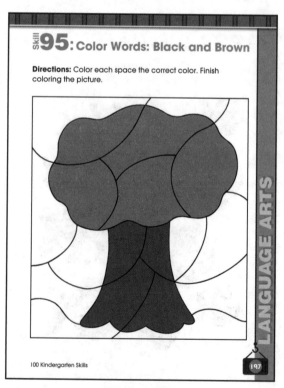

Skill 95: Color Words: Black and Brown

Directions: Color each space the correct color. Finish coloring the picture.

100 Kindergarten Skills

197

Page 197

LANGUAGE ARTS

Answer Key

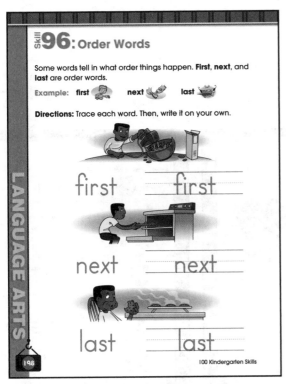

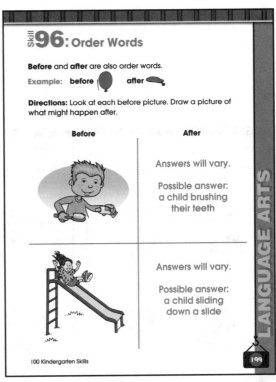

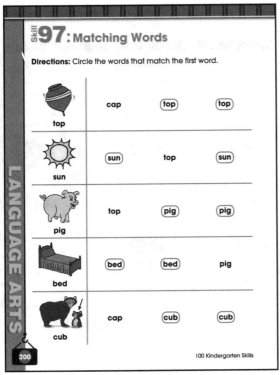

Skill 97: Matching Words

Directions: Circle the words that match the first word.

do	(do)	you	(do)
you	the	(you)	do
sing	you	(sing)	(sing)
the	(the)	you	(the)
cake	(cake)	taste	(cake)

100 Kindergarten Skills

Answer Key

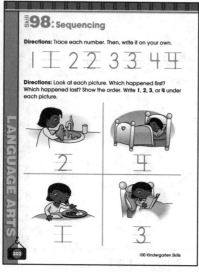

Page 202

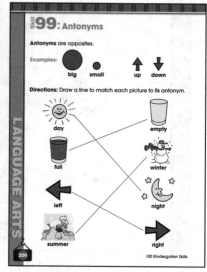

Page 203

Page 204

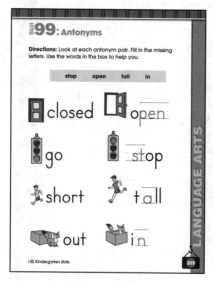

Page 205

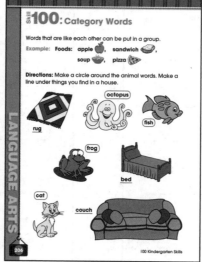

Page 206

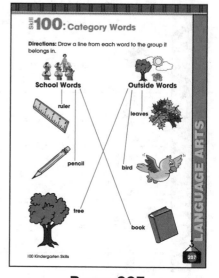

Page 207